THE MAQUIS

THE
MAQUIS

A HISTORY OF THE
FRENCH RESISTANCE MOVEMENT

BY

CLAUDE CHAMBARD

Translated from the French by

ELAINE P. HALPERIN

THE BOBBS-MERRILL COMPANY, INC.

Indianapolis/New York

59573

CONTENTS

CONTENTS

AUTHOR'S PREFACE

Friend, can you hear
The flight of the ravens
Over our plains?

Friend, can you hear
The muffled cry of our country
In chains?

Ah! Partisans,
Workers and peasants,
The alert has sounded.

This evening the enemy
Will learn the price of blood
And of tears.[1]

NO MEMBER OF my generation can remain indifferent to these lines from the *Song of the Partisans* by Maurice Druon.

The eruption of German, then Japanese, invasions during World War II precipitated an unprecedented expansion of that primitive form of military action known as guerrilla warfare. It featured extremely mobile, often poorly armed small groups operating on a terrain thoroughly familiar to them. Almost always, their lightning thrusts enabled them to take the enemy by surprise.

---

1. "Ami, entends-tu
   Le vol noir des corbeaux
   Sur nos plaines?

The multiplicity of their actions was aimed at wearing down the adversary, morally as well as physically. Often the enemy retaliated by subjecting the civilian population to reprisals. But these only strengthened the resistance movement. The intended victims joined the movement, thus increasing its moral influence as well as its membership.

During World War II, guerrilla fighting flared on every front: in France, in the Balkans and the Ukraine, in Burma, in the Philippines, and so on. Its methods, as old as humanity, were systematized and scientifically applied, especially by the Communists, who for several decades had shown the greatest interest in guerrilla warfare.

On the very morrow of World War II we witnessed the spread of guerrilla fighting in Asia, Africa, and South America—at times even among student demonstrators in western non-Communist nations.

It is quite evident that guerrilla warfare can be employed in peacetime as well as in war. It can be directed from without as well as from within. It can be waged at home against a national army as well as against an army of occupation.

Many military experts believe that in a future conflict this type of warfare may supplant more conventional methods, which will have to be discarded because of the balance of terror.

The history of guerrilla warfare is therefore of capital importance for the future. The object of the ensuing chapters is to recount some of the heroic deeds performed during a dramatic period, to relate anecdotes that will evoke the atmosphere of

---

"Ami, entends-tu
Les cris sourds du pays
Qu'on enchaine?

"Ohé! Partisans,
Ouvriers et paysans,
C'est l'alarme.

"Ce soir l'ennemi
Connaitra le prix du sang
Et des larmes."

those days, and finally to assemble facts that will help us to understand more fully the nature of this kind of conflict.

It goes without saying that it is not possible, within the limits of a single volume, to give a completely comprehensive account of the French Resistance. Everywhere, however, we find identical phenomena and identical reactions. We have described some of the most characteristic episodes in an era which, although occasionally diverted from its true purpose by unworthy acts, was on the whole a period of unselfishness and true heroism.

THE MAQUIS

CHAPTER ONE

~~~~~~~

RESISTANCE
BEGINS

IN THE MIDDLE of June 1940 the people of France were con-
fronted for the first time with two irreconcilable responses to
the fact of German conquest. Formal surrender was still a few
days away, but the invaders had taken Paris and overrun all but
the central and southeastern regions of France. On the night of
June 16 a government headed by eighty-five-year-old Marshal
Pétain was formed in Bordeaux. Soon after midnight the Marshal
addressed the nation by radio:

"Sure of the affection of our admirable army, which fought
with traditional heroism against an enemy superior in both numbers and weapons; convinced that it has fulfilled its duties to our
Allies by its magnificent resistance; certain of the full support
of all the veterans whom I have been privileged to command,
and possessing the confidence of all the people, I now dedicate
myself personally to the cause of France in order to alleviate
her misfortunes. . . . It is with heavy heart that I now say to you:

we must try to put an end to the fighting. Tonight I have contacted the enemy to ask if they are prepared to join us, as honorable soldiers, in seeking . . . the means whereby hostilities will be terminated."

The French armies had been pulverized. Civilians clogged the roads, seeking precarious safety, pursuing an illusory hope. Crushed, harassed, demoralized, the French people had but one aspiration: to live in peace once again, to regroup, to restore their broken homes.

And so it was that Frenchmen listened with only half an ear on June 18 when General Charles de Gaulle made his first broadcast to them from London. Speaking on the BBC, he told his countrymen:

The men who for many years led the French armies have now formed a new government. Alleging the defeat of our armies, this government has contacted the enemy to bring a halt to the battle. To be sure, we have been and are overwhelmed by the strength of the enemy—their ground, air, and mechanized units. But far more than numerical superiority, it was German tanks, planes and tactics that pushed us back. It was the tanks, planes, and tactics of the Germans that surprised our leaders and brought them to the place they now find themselves. But has the last word been said? Should all hope be abandoned? Is our defeat final? No!

Believe me, I know what I am talking about when I say that nothing is lost for France. The same means that defeated us can one day bring us victory. For France is not alone! She is not alone! She is not alone! She has behind her a vast empire. She can join forces with the British, who rule the seas and are continuing the struggle. Like England, France can make unlimited use of the immense industrial resources of the United States. The war is not confined to the territory of our unhappy country. The outcome of the war has not been decided by the battle of France. In spite of all the mistakes, all the delays and suffering, there remain in the universe adequate means for the ultimate annihilation of our enemies.

Struck down today by a mechanized force, we shall, in the future, prevail, with the aid of a superior mechanized force. Therein rests the fate of the world.

I, General de Gaulle, presently in London, call upon French officers and enlisted men who happen to be on British soil or who may come here, with or without weapons; I call upon French engineers and workers skilled in weapons industries who happen to be on British soil or who may come here, to put themselves in contact with me. For no matter what happens, the flame of French resistance must not and will not be extinguished.

De Gaulle's brave summons had come at a time when France was neither psychologically nor materially prepared to respond to it. Most of the men old enough to bear arms, together with their officers, had been either killed or taken prisoner. More than 100,000 were dead; two million prisoners had been transported to Germany. In addition, the country was traumatized by the collapse of the Third Republic, which had officially been supplanted by the government headed by Pétain on July 10, 1940. The nation handed over to Marshal Pétain and to the regime established at Vichy the functions and responsibilities of a state that was largely at the mercy of the German occupation forces. For a while, at least, it would seem that France was Pétainist.

But the first signs of resistance began to appear even then in daring individual acts. There were men like Edmond Michelot, a food salesman who, as early as June 1940, had tracts printed in Brive calling for rebellion; or Pierre Kaan, a professor of philosophy at Montluçon who in July went out at night to plaster the walls of the town with circulars inveighing against Hitler and defeat. Sabotage began at the same time. For instance, the newspaper *Ouest Eclair* noted that on July 28, 1940, cable and telephone lines had been cut at Rennes and Fougères. *La France de Bordeaux au Sud-Ouest* confirmed that on August 3, near Angers, a German army long-distance cable had been cut in several places.

A bitter taste of what lay in store for resisters was not long in coming as reprisals also began. For one act of sabotage, the *Feldkommandantur* imposed a fine of two million francs on the city of Nantes. Pierre Roche, an ironmonger from La Rochelle, was arrested by the French police and sentenced to two years in prison for having severed a German telephone wire. Tried by a German military court, he was condemned to death on September 4, 1940, and shot three days later. He had just turned nineteen. A thirty-one-year-old mechanic from Rennes, Marcel Drossier, was executed on September 17 for a similar offense. Blood was beginning to flow, and the German authorities were inextricably caught up in a deadly conflict.

To the accompaniment of the first fusillades by firing squads, a whole series of harassments and reprisals took place. But the great mass of the people were still preoccupied with the struggle to resume their former existence—or simply to survive. The rubble had to be cleared away in many areas, and refugees had to be repatriated. By the beginning of October, about 3,500,000 people had returned to their homes. This avalanche of refugees created desperate problems of food supply, and thousands faced starvation. The Germans often delayed the return of refugees in order to give priority to their convoys, and they used the demarcation line between the Occupied and Unoccupied Zones as a barrier to the movement of refugees.

Meanwhile, help was certainly not pouring in to General de Gaulle in London. He noted in his *War Memoirs:*

> All in all, whatever the reasons, this almost general failure of French personalities to respond did nothing to augment the credit of my enterprise. For a time I had to postpone the formation of my committee. The fact that so few leaders came discouraged other leaders from coming.

Nor did large numbers of French troops rally around him. Eight days after the June 18 appeal, there were still only a few hundred volunteers, camped in Olympia Hall in London. A division of light mountain infantry, commanded by General Bethouard, had taken up quarters in Trentham Park. De Gaulle succeeded in rallying strong elements of two Foreign Legion battalions plus their leader, Lieutenant-Colonel Magrin-Verneret (known as Monclar), and his aide, Captain Koenig, some two hundred riflemen, two-thirds of a tank company, a few members of artillery, engineer, and communications units, together with several staff and intelligence officers, including the commanding officer, de Conchard, and Captains Dewavrin and Tissier.

General de Gaulle's reception of his new collaborators was often frigid. On July 1 Captain Dewavrin presented himself to the general.

"Are you on the active list or in the reserve?" he was asked.

"On the active list, my general."

"Do you have a staff college certificate?"

"No."

"Your training?"

"The Ecole Polytechnique."

"What did you do before mobilization?"

"I taught the science of fortifications at the special military school in Saint-Cyr."

"Have you any other diplomas? Do you speak English?"

"I have a law degree and speak fluent English, my general."

"Where were you during the war?"

"With the expeditionary corps in Norway."

"Then you must know Tissier. Do you outrank him?"

"I do not, my general."

"All right. You will head the second and third bureaus of my general staff. Good-bye. See you soon."

Captain Dewavrin was to become better known under the cover name "Passy."[1]

The first secret agents of Free France were to adopt the

---

1. *Souvenirs,* by Colonel Passy.

names of Paris metro stations. Thus Duclos became "Saint-Jacques"; Lagier, "Bienvenue"; Beresnikoff, "Corvisart"; Dewavrin, "Passy," and so on.

Newcomers to the game of espionage, they were unaware of the sacrosanct rule that required each man to retain the initials of his real name. But Passy observed: "This disregard for rules adopted by all intelligence services throughout the world baffled the enemy secret police for a few months because they never imagined that we were such novices."

De Gaulle's newly created Intelligence Service possessed little detailed information about what was transpiring in France and therefore needed agents in the field. Since the installation of radio broadcasting stations had not yet begun, it meant that agents would have to reach France without any field assistance. This was no small accomplishment.

The first agent left during the latter part of July. His name was Jacques Mansion. Twenty-six years old, he had been gravely wounded on the French front and had been invalided out of the army. Under the cover name "Jack," he traveled through various regions and returned to England in September aboard a fishing boat. With him he brought maps of the enemy's positions and other valuable data. He left behind an embryonic network of informers whom he had supplied with questionnaires drawn up in London. These questionnaires, devised by the French section of the British Intelligence Service, were chiefly intended to supply the British with information about the German invasion of England that seemed imminent in the summer of 1940.

British reconnaissance flights brought back word of intense activity all along the French side of the Channel. In need of more precise information, the British turned to Free French intelligence. Saint-Jacques (Duclos) and Corvisart (Beresnikoff) volunteered their services.

On August 3 the two men left Portsmouth in a fast launch. At four in the morning, near St. Aubin, they were transferred to a small boat. The adventure narrowly missed ending prematurely when the launch, turning back toward the British coast, raced full speed ahead, attracting the notice of German coastal guards. What saved the situation was the early-morning fog.

The two men sank their boat and began to scale the cliffs at St. Aubin. Because there were still no radio stations, they were carrying crates filled with carrier pigeons, which severely hampered their movements. Coming upon a sentinel, they had to abandon the pigeons in a crevice.

Saint-Jacques completed his mission. In three days he had prepared a map indicating all the enemy installations and troop concentrations along the coast. But he never managed to recover the pigeons—the Germans had discovered them. And so the task of bringing back his information remained.

The launch was scheduled to pick up Corvisart any day from August 8 on, but several attempts to do so failed because of the fog. In desperation, Corvisart entered the Unoccupied Zone, made his way to Spain and from there to Portugal, and at last returned to London on January 15, 1941. Although his arrival had been seriously delayed, the information he brought with him was still useful.

Saint-Jacques took advantage of his enforced stay to travel throughout France, making countless contacts and establishing the basis for the intelligence network known as "Paris J 0 6." He also organized networks to operate out of western France and drew up lists of everything they needed: broadcasting equipment, codes, money. He was able to furnish Passy with an exact picture of clandestine working conditions in France. Saint-Jacques managed to return to England by way of North Africa and Portugal.

At this point, the recruiting of agents was still largely a matter of chance and improvisation. Gilbert Renault, who had reached England on a fishing boat in July 1940, went to see Passy.

"Sit down and hand over your papers," Passy told him.

Renault gave him his identity card and passport. Passy studied them, biting his nails, then asked, "Why all these Spanish visas?"

"I was making a movie about Christopher Columbus."

"You make movies? Your identity card says you're an insurance agent."

"It's an old card."

"Have you ever been in intelligence?"

"No, but I thought I . . ."

He explained that he was a businessman; that he had a good many contacts, some of which might prove useful. On the spur of the moment he added, "I know a lot of actors and singers who do radio shows. Maybe we could set up a code that would make it possible for me to send you messages. I'm sure I could manage to insert them in the texts of plays and songs."

As he has written, "Much later I was to learn that this method had often been used, even in the scores of musicals. No one ever invents anything."

After asking Renault for a few references in London, Passy concluded: "I'll think it over. Leave your address with me. I'll keep your passport and your identity card." He was about to recruit a man who, under various names—Jean Luc, de Roulier, but mainly Rémy—was to become one of Free France's most brilliant agents.[2]

Free France was officially created by the de Gaulle–Churchill agreement of August 7, 1940. The text stipulated that General de Gaulle "should proceed to organize a French force composed of volunteers." This was to include naval, land, and air forces, plus some scientific and technical personnel. It was to be used "against the common enemy" and must "never bear arms against France." The cost of establishing and maintaining this force was to be paid by the British government. The money was to be considered an advance.

From the outset the British and French Intelligence Services were involved in constant competition over the recruitment of

---

2. From the accounts of Colonel Passy and Colonel Rémy in *Mémoires d'un Agent Secret de la France Libre,* France-Empire, 1959.

agents. All foreigners who managed to reach England had to pass through the Patriotic School, an interrogation center run by the British. For days, sometimes for weeks, these men were asked to furnish innumerable details of possible interest to British Intelligence.

Passy noted:

> British Intelligence officers picked out individuals who seemed particularly capable and tried to lure them away from us by using all their charm. Frenchmen were asked if they would eventually be willing to return to France for the accomplishment of secret missions. In lyrical terms, the magnificent heroism of nonuniformed soldiers was extolled. Should the candidate fail to show any advance repugnance for this type of activity, he was then regaled with stories about the legendary excellence of the British Intelligence Service. Some allusion would be made in passing to the fact that de Gaulle likewise had an intelligence service of sorts, but the candidate was given to understand that it was made up of inexperienced people who talked too much and who could accomplish little because they lacked the means to do a decent job. If, despite all this, the volunteer seemed quite determined to join the Free French, the recruiters were careful not to persist and, upon releasing him, very kindly provided the address of our service.

As 1940 drew to a close, Free French Intelligence was able to expand its network in France. In November, Gilbert Renault (Rémy) entered France clandestinely from Spain and began to recruit agents for what later came to be known as the CND (Confrérie Notre-Dame). At Perpignan he made contact with Pierre Fourcaud (Lucas), who was assigned to recruiting in the Unoccupied Zone while Renault worked in the Occupied Zone. Both Fourcaud and Renault were supplied with radio transmitters.

On December 22 the fishing trawler *Marie-Louise* brought two passengers from England to France: Lieutenant-Commander

Honoré d'Estienne d'Orves, who used the name Jean-Pierre Girard, and a nineteen-year-old radio operator known as Marty. D'Estienne d'Orves was commissioned to establish bases for an intelligence network to be called NIMROD. Maurice Barlier, a former salesman, and Jean Doornik, a Parisian of Dutch origin who had retained his parents' nationality but chose to enlist in the Free French Forces, were to serve as his adjutants. Both men had been traveling throughout the Occupied and Unoccupied Zones before the arrival of d'Estienne d'Orves, and both had made many contacts. Barlier introduced his chief to friends in Nantes, especially a Monsieur Le Gigan. D'Estienne d'Orves asked Le Gigan to take charge of the Nantes network and placed the radio operator, Marty, at his disposal.

D'Estienne d'Orves left for Paris to continue his mission there, and the new network began to take shape. But in Nantes tragedy was about to strike. Young Marty was keeping highly questionable company. He went so far as to bring a woman to the very room where he kept the precious radio transmitter that linked the network to London. Such rashness was intolerable. D'Estienne d'Orves decided to send Marty back to London as soon as possible and informed him of this decision on January 20, 1941. During the night of January 21–22, the German counterespionage service sent policemen to the homes of Le Gigan and of André Clément, where d'Estienne d'Orves was staying. Marty had betrayed him.

With Marty's assistance, a trap was laid for the *Marie-Louise,* and it was captured by German patrol vessels. Marty's replacement as radio operator, Jean-Jacques Leprince, was on board. Barely eighteen years old, he had served on a submarine and was one of the first to volunteer for service with the Free French. He managed to destroy his radio and all his papers before his capture.

On February 26 the arrested members of the NIMROD network and the men seized on the *Marie-Louise* were brought to the Cherche-Midi Prison in Paris. To prevent d'Estienne d'Orves from communicating with his comrades, he was put in a cell in the section for women inmates.

Among the Cherche-Midi prisoners, all of them political, was an Englishwoman, Mrs. Mary Lindell, arrested for having organized the first network to help downed R.A.F. pilots reach Spain. She recalled hearing one evening a new voice "that silenced all others, a voice filled with poetry, beauty, courage and faith."[3] And the man whom she identified only much later as d'Estienne d'Orves was saying:

> "My friends, my dear friends, and you, all of you who are here because you are fighting for freedom, listen to me! I have assumed full and total responsibility for everything we have done. I said that I was the one who persuaded all of you to join my network. When you are interrogated, conduct yourselves in a manner worthy of Frenchmen. Remember that you have had the honor of fighting for France, and that you spearheaded the fight even before those of our compatriots who are now in England. A few of us will die. That is inevitable. May God allow us to die honorably! Good night, my friends, courage, and may God help you!"

The trial of Honoré d'Estienne d'Orves and his companions began on May 13, 1941, and lasted for twelve days. D'Estienne d'Orves, Maurice Barlier, Jean Doornik, Le Gigan, André Clément and his wife, Jean-Jacques Leprince, Jean-François Follic (owner of the *Marie-Louise*), and Pierre Cornec (who had guided the boat's passengers to the landing place) were all condemned to death. Doornik was given an additional five years' imprisonment for having attempted to help a volunteer reach England; when the sentence was pronounced, Doornik called out: "Your honor, am I to do my five years after the execution?" The

---

3. *No Drums . . . No Trumpets: The Story of Mary Lindell,* by Barry Wynne, London, 1961.

other prisoners taken at Nantes were sentenced to terms ranging from six months to penal servitude for life.

Not all Germans were indifferent to the lot of the condemned men. Father Frantz Stock, the prisoners' admirable chaplain, proved to be a great help to them. First Lieutenant Johannes Mörner, appointed to serve as d'Estienne d'Orves's lawyer, twice traveled to Berlin to support a motion in favor of mercy which the presiding judge himself had approved. The prosecutor who had prepared the case against the defendants did something similar.

And in the Vichy government, Admiral Darlan personally intervened, addressing himself to General Von Stülpnagel, the German commander-in-chief in France.

Hitler remained adamant with respect to d'Estienne d'Orves, Barlier, and Doornik. But in a rare gesture of mercy designed to encourage French collaboration, he decided to commute the sentences of the other doomed men to hard labor.

Le Gigan has described the execution of the three condemned men: "At dawn on August 29, I was awakened by the sergeant-at-arms, who ordered me to go downstairs immediately (at that time I didn't know that my sentence had been commuted). In the relative darkness of the Fresnes prison, I saw my three friends surrounded by German officers and a firing squad. Count d'Orves had been given permission to say a last farewell to his principal associates, and I was able to embrace him as well as Barlier and Doornik a few moments before their execution. All three died like heroes, refusing to be blindfolded or to have their hands shackled. Standing at attention as they were about to die, they prayed for their families and for France."

The execution took place at Mont Valérien, where 4,500 patriots were later to be shot. It was to become one of the famous landmarks of the Resistance.

While men like d'Estienne d'Orves were being sent from England to establish Resistance operations, groups that had no connections with the London leadership were also being formed.

As early as July 1940, Boris Vildé, a young ethnologist affiliated with the *Musée de l'Homme,* organized a movement whose purpose it was to help escaped prisoners, whether French or Allied, to make their way into the Unoccupied Zone. At the start, Vildé was aided by two colleagues, Anatole Lewitzky, head of the Department of Comparative Technology, and Yvonne Oddon, a librarian. Others were soon to join, most notably several professors and a group of lawyers. By mid-December the Vildé organization was calling itself the "National Committee of Public Safety," or simply "Résistance," after the name of its clandestine newspaper, the first mimeographed issue of which appeared on December 15.

The first issue of *Résistance* launched a powerful and memorable appeal:

Resist! That is the cry that comes from the hearts of all of you, amid the anguish caused by our country's disaster. It is the cry of all who are not resigned, who yearn to perform their duty. But you feel isolated and helpless; you seek the path of duty amid the chaos of ideas, opinions, and systems. To resist is at least to preserve your heart and brain, but above all it is to act, to do something that can be translated into positive accomplishment, into useful and reasonable action. Many have tried, but they have been discouraged by their impotence.

The method? Assemble in your homes with people you know. Choose your leaders, who will then find experienced men to direct your activities and keep you informed through various channels. In order to coordinate your efforts with those of Unoccupied France and of the forces fighting at our side, our committee will issue all the necessary orders. Your immediate task is to organize, so that you will be able to resume the fight the moment you receive the order to do so. Employing careful screening methods, enlist the help of determined men and surround them with even better ones. Lend comfort and courage to those who doubt, who no longer dare to hope. Search out and keep watch over those who have turned their backs on our country and betrayed it. Meet once a day and pass along to your leaders all useful information. Practice rigid discipline, constant prudence, absolute discretion.

In accepting the responsibility of becoming your leaders, we have sworn to sacrifice everything to this mission, ruthlessly and mercilessly.

Unknown to one another yesterday, none of us has ever before participated in the quarrels of prewar political parties, in the deliberations of either legislative bodies or ministries. We are completely independent, Frenchmen and nothing else. We have been chosen because we promise action. We have but a single ambition, one passion, one desire: to restore an undefiled and free France.

But this promising organization was also doomed. In February 1941 it was denounced by a double agent and dismantled by the Germans. The trial of its leaders took place a year later, and ten were condemned to death. Boris Vildé and six other men were executed on February 23, 1942, at Mont Valérien. Three condemned women were sent to Nazi prisons.

Clandestine publishing was an important activity of many of the first Resistance groups. On September 20, 1940, five men met at the home of Alcide Morel, a Parisian bank employee, to discuss the possibilities for taking action. Since the day they met was the anniversary of the victorious battle of Valmy against the Prussians in 1792, the group took the name of "Valmy." In January 1941 they began to publish a clandestine newspaper which was originally printed, in just fifty copies, with equipment purchased at a toy counter. With more professional facilities available to them later, they were able to expand their circulation into the thousands.

Also in September 1940, Captain Henri Frenay and Lieutenant Maurice Chevance met in Marseilles to plan the creation of a secret army to harass the Germans until such a time as it could openly support massive Allied action. In April 1941 in

Lyon, they started a clandestine newsletter titled *Les Petites Ailes*.

Although the Communist Party withheld formal support for the Resistance movement until after the Soviet Union was attacked, its fighting group came into existence at this time. Called *Francs Tireurs et Partisans* (FTP), it was organized in Lyon by Eugene Petit, Antoine Avinin, and Jean-Pierre Lévy.

In December 1940, near Cannes, squadron leader Corniglion-Molinier, former naval officer Emmanuel d'Astier de la Vigerie, and Albert Kohan formed a propaganda group called La Dernière Colonne.

A group of Christian Democrats spread the word among students and others, using the newspaper *Liberté* as their official organ. Soon this group also began to form commando units.

What were to become major Resistance groups were being organized in every section of France. General de Gaulle, meanwhile, despite the formidable obstacles and rebuffs he first encountered, was gradually strengthening his leadership and enlarging the role of his forces in support of the Resistance movement.

CHAPTER TWO

~~~~~~~~

EARLY
ACTION

THE "ACTION" BRANCH of the Free French Intelligence Service came into being late in 1940. Captain Bergé and some thirty other French volunteers whom he had recruited first received training as parachutists, and next, at a large estate north of London, they were instructed in all the techniques of sabotage. "It was then that we were to discover for the first time the destructive power of plastic bombs," Bergé recalled.[1]

The difficulties the new group faced were brought home in some of their early operations. One morning in February 1941, Captain Bergé was told to select an officer and a few men to parachute into France. Their mission: to attack and destroy a bus transporting German army pilots at the Meucon airfield near Vannes. The R.A.F. was interested in these men because they were a pathfinder force that specialized in nighttime aerial

---

1. General Bergé's testimony in *Historia Magazine, World War II,* no. 31.

bombing. It was these pilots who spearheaded the nightly bombing of England by lighting up the objectives with target-marking fires.

The mission, christened "Savannah," commenced on March 15. Bergé was accompanied by Second Lieutenant Petit-Laurent, Master Sergeants Forman and Joël Le Tac, and Corporal Renault. Unfortunately, their pilot lost his way, and the men were dropped some eight kilometers from the designated point. For three days they dragged around their infernal container of explosives, a load of over forty kilos, only to discover in the end that the bus no longer followed the route given in their month-old information.

Before returning to England, aboard the British submarine *Tigris,* Bergé managed to organize a network of cells in Bordeaux, Bayonne, and the Landes that would be on hand to pick up parachutists. Since one of the canoes designed to bring the team to the submarine had been smashed, Joël Le Tac was obliged to give up his place and go on to Paris.

On May 11 Sergeant Forman parachuted again, this time over Bordeaux, with Second-Lieutenants Varnier and Cabard on a mission called "Josephine B." The three carried a magnetic case of incendiary bombs to be attached to the walls of the transformers at the Pessac power station—an objective difficult to reach by air. The explosion was to be set off by means of a detonator, and destruction would be completed by incendiary grenades that were to set fire to the oil in the transformers.

On spotting their objective, the three men were dismayed to find a high-tension wire along the top of the boundary wall. And they could hear people moving about inside the power station. They lost heart and gave up, but missed the submarine they were to have boarded near Mimizan for the return trip. Eventually, however, they found Joël Le Tac in Paris.

Led by Le Tac, the "Josephine" team returned to Bordeaux. This time the operation was successful. On June 7 six of the eight transformers were destroyed. Le Tac noted: "Repairs on them could not be completed until the following year, so steam trains had to be reintroduced to keep the line on the southwest railway going. Moreover, activities at the submarine base in Bordeaux and the operation of many factories had to be suspended for several weeks."

This was the first successful act of sabotage by a French team organized in England. In reprisal, the municipality of Pessac was fined a million francs, and a curfew was imposed.

Clandestine radio facilities were by now operating satisfactorily, but careful coordination was needed in arranging parachute drops. "Blind" drops had proved too risky. Steps had to be taken to ensure that both personnel and equipment would be dropped over a lighted air strip.

Agents were trained to select suitable landing areas—fields free of obstacles, not too far from wooded areas where containers could be buried after their contents had been removed. At the time of a drop, agents were to place on the field three lighted flares in the shape of a triangle, taking into account the direction of the wind. With the aid of a flashlight or special torch, they were to use previously agreed on Morse code signals to the planes making the drop.

The rendezvous scenario went something like this: the head of a network would be informed by radio from London to prepare for a drop of equipment or men on a certain date, which would be given a code name. On that day, if the operation could proceed as planned, the Free French Intelligence Service would send over the BBC several successive coded messages containing the phrase that would notify the head of the network to alert his reception committee and to go to the appropriate landing strip. If, at the last minute, all plans had to be canceled (weather conditions often necessitated a last-minute switch), the code phrase would be omitted from the 9:30 P.M. broadcast and replaced by a message signifying that the plane could not leave until the next day. Several variations of this communication system were devised in order to confuse the enemy, but in all essential respects it was employed throughout the war.

The air drops of men and equipment coming from England to France made possible a fairly satisfactory liaison in this direction. But traffic also had to flow the other way. Whenever secret agents had "blown their cover," they had to be evacuated with dispatch. The number of downed flyers picked up by the networks constantly grew and since these men were a burden and a serious danger to anyone who hid them, it was important to get them back as quickly as possible. Some reached Spain after a long and difficult trip through the Pyrenees. Others tried to return to England by boat, but the coasts were well patrolled, and the attempt was always hazardous. It was therefore necessary to arrange pickups by light planes that could land at night. This involved careful selection in advance of any and all possible landing strips. The mission of designating these strips, called "Brick," was entrusted to Lieutenant Mitchell, who was dropped in France on June 19, 1941.

Mitchell looked for flat strips about 650 yards long, with a clearing on every side so that within a 1,200-square-yard radius there would be no obstacle exceeding a height of two and a half yards. Such strips were not easy to find in France.

The plane used for these secret missions was almost always the Westland "Lysander," a single-engine, high-wing monoplane. Produced in 1936, it had a cruising speed of 165 miles per hour. It could land and take off over a stretch of 500 to 600 yards. It rarely spent more than two minutes on the ground, discharging and receiving its passengers.

All radio transmissions were carefully monitored by the Germans, who used pathfinder techniques to locate clandestine wireless sets. Colonel Rémy recalled the tragic outcome for one radioman, Bernard Anquetil, in the summer of 1941.

On July 29 Rémy went to Saumur to send a message over Anquetil's transmitter.

"I'm a little worried," Anquetil told Rémy.[2] "Yesterday I saw a radio-equipped car crossing the bridge, and German civilians come here to eat in my restaurant."

"You'll have to stop transmitting," Rémy replied. "You've done a lot of work these last few days, and it wouldn't be surprising if the enemy has begun to take an interest and is trying to find out what you're up to. Let me find out where I can hide you."

Anquetil protested: "Listen, Monsieur, I don't think there's anything seriously wrong. Give me your message. I'll send it out tomorrow at ten."

And so, the earphones clamped around his head, he transmitted Rémy's message. While he was at it, three radio squads surrounded the entire block of buildings. Anquetil, although taken by surprise, managed to destroy his set by tossing it out of the window. He was tortured by the Gestapo but never talked. They shot him that October. Another radio operator was arrested a little later, near Rouen. But in spite of such cruel losses, the networks expanded, and their influence spread over all of France.

---

2. *Mémoires d'un Agent de la France Libre,* by Colonel Rémy, France-Empire, 1959.

CHAPTER THREE

EARLY
REPRISALS

THE GERMAN ATTACK on the Soviet Union profoundly altered certain aspects of the Resistance in France. Until June 21, 1941, the Communist Party as an organization was inactive in the Resistance movement because of its support for the Nazi-Soviet Pact. Only a few of its members, acting on a purely individual basis, had joined the Free French.

The party maintained a large clandestine press, organized defense groups, and actively opposed the Vichy government, with consequent reprisals. But on the political level, the Communists condemned the war, contending that it was a struggle between rival imperialists. They denounced General de Gaulle and all those who had responded to his appeal as "dangerous warmongers in the pay of England."

With the Nazi invasion of Russia, on June 22, everything changed. Not only did the Communists rally to the side of the "warmongers," they also introduced a new style of combat.

While the Gaullist networks had done their best to avoid violence
for fear of mass reprisals, the Communists advocated drastic
measures. Acts of sabotage multiplied, and attacks against German soldiers and collaborators became especially frequent.

On August 15 General von Stülpnagel, the German commander-in-chief in France, issued a warning to every inhabitant:

"Since the French Communist Party has been dissolved, all
Communist activity in France is forbidden. Anyone who par-
ticipates in a Communist-inspired action, who spreads Communist propaganda or tries to do so, in short, anyone who in
any way supports the machinations of Communists, will be considered dangerous. All guilty persons will be subject to the death
penalty, which will be pronounced by a German court-martial.
Any person who comes across anti-German tracts must hand
them over immediately to the nearest German military post.
Those who disobey will be sentenced to up to fifteen years of
hard labor. I expect everyone to act in accordance with the
dictates of wisdom and common sense, and to continue to prevent irresponsible elements from supporting the enemies of Germany. And I must warn you of the grave consequences that
could result from the hostile attitude of Communists, not only
for the guilty persons themselves, but also for the entire population of the occupied country."

On August 21 an incident occurred which was a perfect
example of futile violence. Gilbert Brustlein has recounted the
story:[1]

> One day, in front of the Gare de Lyon, I saw a German
> officer going up the stairs. I hurried up after him to settle his
> hash. My companions grabbed my arm. "It's impossible to do
> anything right now," they admonished. But Fabien would not
> listen. "Good God, I'll show you what we've got to do!" he said
> It didn't take him long. At eight o'clock we caught up with

---

1. *La Résistance et les Communistes,* by Colonel R. du Jonchay, France
   Empire, 1968.

him in the Barbès-Rochouart Metro station. He gave each of us an assignment: my comrade was to keep an eye on the quais, mixing with the crowd; I was to protect him, for he was planning an assassination.

Suddenly, a German naval officer entered the Metro corridor and headed toward an incoming train. Fabien muttered: "Careful, that's the one." Just as the officer was about to step into the first-class carriage, Fabien fired two bullets into his back, turned on his heel, and made for the stairs leading to the exit.

The victim of this pointless assassination was Midshipman Mozer. The German authorities reacted with a brutal decree: 'First, from August 23 on, all Frenchmen who have been arrested will be considered hostages. Second, should there be another such episode, a number of hostages, depending upon the gravity of the act, will be shot."

General de Gaulle did not favor such isolated acts. In his *War Memoirs* he had this to say:

> It was with somber pride that we learned of these acts of war committed by individuals at great personal risk, against the occupying army. . . . For elementary reasons of combat tactics, we believed that the struggle should be properly directed and that, moreover, the time had not yet come to commence open warfare in Metropolitan France.

The attacks continued nevertheless, and reprisals multiplied. On September 16, another decree was plastered over the walls of Paris:

> On September 6 and 11, 1941, acts of violence were committed in Paris against members of the German army. By way of reprisal for such cowardly attacks, and in accordance with my decree of August 22, 1941, the following hostages have been shot: Matheron, Lucien; Joly, René; Clément, Lucien; Gokelvere, Albert; Bonnin, André; Libermann, David; Mager, Opal

Chil; Bernheim, Isidore; Bekermann, Henri; Blum, Lucien.
Signed: General von Stülpnagel.

A large proportion of the population took such news quite
calmly. The fact that no potatoes could be found anywhere at
the time apparently made more of an impression on one citizen
who concluded, "Naturally, we're being deprived of them because Germans are being assassinated."

The truth was that eating, simply eating enough to prevent
hunger, had become an obsession in a country where the black
market was gradually affecting every region. Prices increased at
a staggering rate. The only way to supplement the average mea-
ger rations was to engage in black or "parallel" market deals, if
one were in a position to do so. For the unfortunates who did
not have the means, famine was a constant threat.

While the population was struggling with such daily diffi-
culties, often indifferent to the London- or Moscow-inspired
Resistance, the tragedy of hostages loomed ever larger. On
December 21 Marshal Pétain addressed his countrymen in the
Occupied Zone:

> I must tell you tonight, with deep emotion and total sin-
> cerity, how we must regard the repeated attacks that have been
> perpetrated in recent weeks against individual members of the
> army of occupation. These are criminal acts. And they can only
> bring us further misfortune. This must be the work of foreign
> agents, for underhanded attacks against soldiers who are merely
> carrying out orders are not compatible with our French traditions.
> Your government officially condemns this and will attempt, with
> every means at its disposal, to uncover the culprits. I ask you to
> give us every assistance. If we allow such criminal acts to con-
> tinue, we shall risk reprisals against innocent people, in spite of
> all my efforts to avoid them. Frenchmen in the Occupied Zone, I
> am fully aware of your sentiments. Your ordeal and your anguish
> affect me deeply. But do not forget that the misfortunes of our
> country call for exceptional and unwavering responsibility toward

the nation as a whole. Your first duty, in every eventuality, is to safeguard whatever is conducive to the unity of France. Such unity requires above all, as you yourselves must realize, the maintenance of order. I rely upon you to insure the unity of our country with order and dignity.

Pierre Pucheu, the Vichy government's minister of the interior, journeyed to Paris to apprise General von Stülpnagel of the measures the French authorities were taking to prevent "terrorist" attacks. He also went, however, to denounce as "despicable" the assassination of "completely innocent" hostages. From his interviews with the head of the army of occupation, Pucheu came away with the impression that Stülpnagel was carrying out the dictates of Hitler and his chief of staff, Field Marshal Keitel.

Keitel commented later on the subject of reprisals:

> To German officers who had been reared with the concept of a "chivalrous war," we were obliged to emphasize the fact that when you are dealing with an enemy who employs such methods, you must not hesitate to retaliate in kind if you wish to remain in control of the situation. . . . But the German is by nature so easygoing that he sometimes allows the roof over his head to burn down before he is convinced that there is any danger of a fire.

He summed up the official German view of the situation in France:

> At first the French police made a serious effort to put an end to acts of sabotage and to punish the culprits in order to eliminate this danger. However, they soon behaved very differently, thereby revealing their sympathy for the authors of such reprehensible acts. This demonstrated not only that the orders came from above; it also proved that the underground warfare against the occupying forces was being systematically directed.

The consequences, according to Keitel, were grave:

We had to appeal ever more urgently for reinforcements of our police and security services. The taking of hostages and the resort to other kinds of reprisals likewise became an absolute necessity for us. But since the Balkans, too, required reinforcements, and occupied territories in Russia were constantly demanding the kind of intensified surveillance for which our depleted security forces were well known to be inadequate, the Führer prescribed reprisals in order to create a salutary atmosphere of fear. We had to act with the greatest dispatch in order to avoid being overrun. We had to strike to prevent the resistance movements from using their increasing numbers to threaten the authority of the occupying forces.

During the summer and autumn of 1941 we began to issue directives designed to put a stop to this modern type of guerrilla warfare. . . . The underground was at first directed by obscure men from such bodies as the British Secret Service, and its work was mainly done by paid secret agents, by criminals of every kind, by rabble with no beliefs or respect for the law. Later they were joined by men of a certain idealism, and today their acts are glorified as the deeds of so-called "patriots."

Keitel was attempting to justify his signature on the infamous "Night and Fog" order of December 7, 1941. This order decreed the instant execution of all non-German civilians found guilty of "criminal acts against the Reich or the occupation authorities." If it proved impossible to impose the death sentence through the courts in occupied territory, the offenders were to be transported without delay to the Reich for punishment. Beyond the mere announcement of their arrest, no news about the fate of such deportees would be provided—hence the name "Night and Fog."

From the names of the victims on reprisal execution lists, it was obvious that a large number of Jews were being included. Ever since the June 1940 armistice, an anti-Semitic campaign had been under way throughout both Occupied and Unoccupied France.

As early as September 1940, a census was taken of Jews in the Occupied Zone, and the occupation authorities issued a decree obliging every Jewish shopkeeper to place a sign in his window reading "Jewish enterprise." On April 26, 1941, Jews were forbidden to engage in "certain" activities, including wholesale and retail sales, restaurants, hotels, transportation, and banks. Furthermore, Jews could no longer be employed in enterprises where they "would come in contact with the public." On May 29, 1942, every Jew from the age of six upward was ordered to wear a yellow star stamped with the word "Jew."

By May 1941, 3,200 Jews were interned in camps at Pithiviers and Beaune-la-Rolande within the Occupied Zone. For the most part, they were men who had volunteered in 1939 to fight the Germans.

In the Unoccupied Zone, the situation evolved more slowly. At first the Vichy authorities pursued Jews of foreign origin, whom they were all too ready to blame for anything and everything. Entire communities of Jews, expelled from the Palatinate and Baden, had flocked to France, swelling the number of stateless persons. In October 1940 these foreign Jews were interned at Gurs. Conditions there were appalling, as Chief Rabbi Joseph Kaplan has testified:[2]

> Crowded together in barracks, the Jews slept on the ground. Devoured by vermin, they also suffered from hunger and cold in the muddy, humid region. During the winter of 1940–41 alone, 800 of them died. In January 1941 families with children were sent to Rivesaltes in the eastern Pyrenees, but the situation there was scarcely any better.

A letter from the rabbi addressed to Xavier Vallat, head of the Vichy Commissariat-General of Jewish Affairs, was answered in a most curious way by Jarnieu, Vallat's chief of staff:

> You have cited certain facts that are quite well known and which would not have been denied by the French parliament

---

2. Quoted in *La Résistance Juive en France*, by David Knout.

because our land has been invaded by such large numbers of Jews during the last few years, people who have no affinity with our French civilization. I have no intention of refuting in detail some of your allegations, especially your statistics about the number of Jews in the army who died for France. That is a subject too deserving of our respect to be made an object of contention. I will simply confine myself to saying that the government harbors no anti-Semitism, that it acts solely out of consideration for reasons of state.

It was in the name of "reasons of state" that Jews and Communists were being tracked down with increasing vigor. Individual attacks on the Germans continued to multiply, and these were swiftly followed by reprisals.

On October 20 events took another tragic turn. In Nantes a group of *Francs-Tireurs* blew up a length of railway track and then went to the center of town and shot the German field commander, Lieutenant-Colonel Hotz. The next day in Bordeaux, an officer in the German administration, Councilor Reimers, was killed under similar circumstances. On October 22 the Germans shot forty-eight hostages. Twenty-seven of them had been interned in the Châteaubriant detention camp, including seventeen-year-old Guy Môquet, son of a Communist deputy from Paris, Pierre Môquet, who was then in an Algerian prison. The boy was arrested toward the end of 1940 for demonstrating against the occupying forces and joining his fellow classmates at the Lycée Carnot to distribute leaflets. He was acquitted but not freed. From the Santé prison he was transferred to the jail at Clairvaux and subsequently taken to Châteaubriant. On the morning of October 22, Madame Kérival, whose husband was among the hostages to be executed, offered to die in Guy Môquet's place. The Germans refused. In spite of his courage, the young boy fainted at the moment of execution, and he was virtually unconscious when his body was riddled with German bullets.

Fifty more hostages were slated for execution. Pétain sent

Pierre Pucheu to Paris to intervene on their behalf. "I went to Paris," the minister recounted, "and for three hours I pleaded with the Germans. I warned General von Stülpnagel that Marshal Pétain himself and his ministers would travel to the demarcation line and offer themselves as hostages if he refused to cancel the executions. He finally gave in."[3]

On October 23, in a radio address from London, General de Gaulle took the following position:

"It is absolutely natural and justifiable for Frenchmen to kill Germans. If the Germans do not wish to die by our hands, they have only to return to their own country. . . . Since they have failed to bring ruin to the universe, they can be certain that they will soon become either corpses or prisoners. . . . But there is such a thing as war tactics. War must be conducted by those in charge of it. . . . For the moment, I am ordering our people in the Occupied Zone not to kill Germans openly, and this for only one reason: right now it is too easy for the enemy to retaliate by slaughtering our fighters, who are not yet armed. But as soon as we are in a position to attack, the order you desire will be given."

Then he asked all Frenchmen, "wherever they may happen to be, to halt all activities and stand at attention from four until four zero five on Friday, October 31. This massive gesture, this immense national strike, will disclose to the enemy the threat that hangs over them. It will also serve to demonstrate French solidarity."

His request was complied with, and the head of the Free French subsequently noted:

> It strengthened my resolve to prevent the Resistance from falling into a state of anarchy. Rather, I would strive to forge it into an organized whole, without, however, destroying the spirit of initiative that inspired it, nor the framework without which it might suddenly cease to exist.

---

3. It was on October 30 that Hitler granted the fifty hostages a reprieve *sine die*.

CHAPTER FOUR

MOVING
TO UNITE

AT THE END of 1941, three of the principal Resistance groups of the Unoccupied Zone were exploring the possibility of joining forces and identifying themselves with General de Gaulle. The Free French Intelligence Service had widened its contacts with the Resistance movement in the north as well as in the south, and the year 1942 was notable for the organizing activities of a leading de Gaulle representative and great Resistance fighter, Jean Moulin.

As prefect in Chartres in 1940, Jean Moulin gave proof of his extraordinary energy and courage. Confronting the occupation authorities under highly dramatic circumstances, he drew admiration even from German officers. Dismissed by the Vichy government, he went to live in Saint-Andiol in the Bouches-du-Rhône, near Avignon, using his leisure in this retreat to make contact with all kinds of people.

When he decided to go to London, Moulin succeeded in

getting out of France by fabricating his own travel papers, using the name of one Joseph-Jean Mercier, a law professor at an American university. Armed with authorization to "return" to the United States by way of Spain and Portugal, he left France on September 12, 1941, and made his way via Lisbon to England in October.

After putting him through a tough examination, the British Intelligence Service tried to recruit him. Alerted, de Gaulle intervened. "Thanks to a pressing letter addressed to Mr. Eden," the General later recalled, "I managed to see that the loyal traveler reached his true destination. I subsequently encountered at least as many difficulties in arranging for his return to France."

On January 1, 1942, at four in the morning, Jean Moulin was dropped near Saint-Andiol. Three men parachuted from the Whitley two-engine plane: Moulin; Air Force Lieutenant Fassim who was to put him in contact with the *Combat* Resistance group; and a radio operator, Montjaret. Owing to a miscalculation, the pilot went off course and dropped the men ten miles from their intended destination. Moulin sank up to his knees in a marsh and was injured, but he managed to extricate himself. And so, under the most trying circumstances, this forty-three-year-old art connoisseur and talented sketcher began his fabled career as a secret agent.

In the false bottom of a matchbox, Moulin carried a microfilm containing the orders for his mission signed in de Gaulle's own hand. Dated December 24, 1941, the document stated: "I hereby appoint Monsieur M. J. Moulin, prefect, as my representative and delegate to the National Committee for the zone in metropolitan France that is not directly occupied. Monsieur Moulin's mission is to coordinate all the activities of the various groups in the zone that are resisting the enemy and its collaborators. He will report the results of his mission directly to me."

It was often difficult for Moulin to establish the necessary contacts. Emmanuel d'Astier de la Vigerie, chief of Liberation, sent Aubrac, his second-in-command, to see him, but when

Moulin presented his microfilmed orders, Aubrac refused to accept them as "proof of authority." Things went more smoothly when he contacted Henri Frenay of *Combat,* the name by which the Resistance fusion movement was known. Guillain de Bénouville, who was present at the meeting, at Marcelle Bidault's house in Marseilles, has described it: "In the kitchen, Jean Moulin took out a handwritten letter and placed it on the drainboard. No one said a word. A handwritten letter from General de Gaulle! Then he gave us the orders from London."

The very nature of the mission aroused a certain amount of suspicion. Frenay noted: "These orders were not consistent with the framework within which we had been operating. Whereas we wished to retain our own initiative, the orders were precise and rigid down to the smallest detail."

Moulin turned over to Frenay 250,000 francs, half of the total amount he had been given in London. As head of a major Resistance movement, Frenay needed money as well as a liaison with London. His activities, though clandestine, were not unknown to Vichy. Several members of *Combat* had been arrested. In January 1942 Pierre Pucheu, Minister of the Interior, summoned Frenay to demand that he cease his attacks against Marshal Pétain. But he did not ask him to give up his clandestine activities against the Germans. On the contrary, Frenay was given a pass, valid for two weeks, to show to the French police. And at a second interview with Pucheu he obtained a similar pass that was good for a month.

Even in Vichy at that time there were efforts to resist the occupiers. The Vichy government's Intelligence Service displayed a keen interest in everything the Germans did. In masterly fashion, it succeeded in tapping the Paris-Berlin telephone line, used by both the civil and the military authorities as their main communications link with the capital of the Reich. An instrument made in the Unoccupied Zone was transported piece by piece to a cottage at Noisy-le-Grand and attached by way of a tunnel from the basement to the Paris-Berlin cable. By the beginning of January 1942, the tapping system, known in intelligence circles as "Source K," was functioning. Pertinent information was relayed to Vichy by employees of the Post and Telegraph Services, or by waiters working in railway dining cars. "Source K" functioned until Christmas Eve, 1942, when one of its operators was surprised while at work by a Wehrmacht team that was hunting for billets. The two others happened to be absent at the moment, managed to escape, and were later smuggled to safety via Spain.

Frenchmen had ever more urgent need to know what was happening at German headquarters as the occupation became more cruelly repressive. At the time of the invasion of France in June 1940, there had been no sign of Himmler's *Einsatzgruppen* (extermination teams). Their most fortunate absence was due solely to the fact that they were busy committing atrocities in Poland. Actually, the German High Command was opposed to the presence of Gestapo combat or security police teams when the Wehrmacht marched into Paris. But Himmler was tenacious. Bypassing the decisions of the German military, he succeeded in establishing in Paris a small Gestapo unit.

These first special or autonomous commandos were led by an S.S. major, Helmut Knochen, a doctor of philosophy, intelligent and outwardly amiable. His men were mainly young off-shoots of the *Ausland* security police and specialists in French affairs. At first they worked with the German military police, to whom they appealed whenever they wanted an arrest made. A second, then a third team soon appeared.

Although he was very shrewd, Knochen soon encountered the hostility of General von Stülpnagel. Organized attacks against Jewish synagogues in October 1941 did nothing to improve relations between the two men. The general learned that these deeds were perpetrated by two Frenchmen, Eugène Deloncle and Jean Filliol, with the connivance of the Gestapo. Stülpnagel appealed to Heydrich himself but failed to obtain the recall of Knochen, who was too valuable a man for the Nazis to dispense with.

Early in 1942 the Germans considered the idea of placing a Gauleiter at the head of the French government. They believed that the policy of collaboration was a fiasco and were convinced that administrative questions should be settled in France in exactly the same way as they had been handled in Poland, Holland, and Norway. Names were already being suggested: the Prince von Würtemberg, von Papen.

Despite German misgivings about him, on April 18, 1942, Pierre Laval again became head of the Vichy government, replacing Admiral Darlan, who was appointed commander-in-chief of the land, sea and air forces. To explain the reshuffle, Pétain made the following radio announcement:

"Today, at a moment as decisive as June 1940, I am joining Monsieur Pierre Laval to begin the national work of European reconstruction for which together we have laid the foundations. Frenchmen, the new government will give you fresh reason to have faith and to hope."

The Germans gave up the idea of appointing a Reich Commissioner for France, but they nevertheless made important changes designed to reinforce their police system. Hitler took away from the German army its police powers in France and entrusted them to S.S. Brigadier-General Karl Albrecht Oberg, one of Heydrich's principal associates. Heydrich came to Paris to introduce Oberg to the authorities. During the course of a ceremony at the Ritz Hotel, he detailed the extent of Oberg's authority:

> General Oberg is to be responsible for everything that affects public order and internal security in the Occupied Zone. In discharging his mission, he will be aided by the German police as well as by the divisions of the S.S. The French administration must comply with all relevant orders issued by the German authorities. Such obedience is properly due to the occupying power.

Oberg quickly unified the German police force, organizing it into two groups: a force to maintain order (*Ordnungspolizei,*

or Orpo) and security police (*Sicherheitspolizei,* or Sipo SD),
the latter of which remained under the command of Knochen,
who was promoted to colonel. Regional services were enlarged,
and seven new divisions were created. Moreover, each division
had a great many local police stations at its disposal as well as
agents in even the smallest towns.

Three Gestapo services employed Frenchmen: Intervention-
Referat, Section IV of the emergency police squad, and the
Chamberlin-Bony group. The first was made up of shock troops
belonging to Jacques Doriot's *Parti Populaire Français* and of
men who were members of a Marseilles criminal gang. The
second consisted of Frenchmen who were already working for
the Gestapo and had been especially trained for service of this
kind. The third, organized by Bony and a former quartermaster
of the police prefecture, one Lafon, alias Chamberlin, was
manned exclusively by offenders who had been condemned in
the law courts.

Resistance forces soon felt the impact of the German police
reorganization. "The conventional phase of repression was followed by total repression," Michel Garder later recalled.[1]

> German security S.S. officers were determined to prove to
> those bourgeois Abwehr and G.F.P. [Geheime Feld Polizei] func-
> tionaries that their old-fashioned methods had failed. Recourse to
> violence and medieval torture became the rule. Spurning military
> justice, the German S.D. gave the courts only hand-picked
> "clients." For all the others, the "slow death" camps served both
> as jails and as places of extermination.

With the cooperation of Vichy, German persecution of the
Jews was intensified. On July 12, a circular distributed by the
director of the Paris municipal police, Hennequin, ordered massive new arrests and deportation of Jews. For it was the French
police who were called on to discharge this barbarous task. Eight

---

1. *La Guerre secrète des Services Spéciaux Français.*

hundred and eighty-eight arresting teams totaling 9,000 men performed the job. Even police cadets were pressed into service, with an eye to giving them some practical experience. It must be said, however, that no one in France realized what the Germans had in mind. No person in his right mind could then conceive what the "final solution" meant.

The Germans thought of everything. They set up a General Union of Israelites in France, camouflaged as an emergency mutual aid organization. Jews seeking work came here and left their names. On the morning of July 15, a number of these unemployed were called in by the General Union and asked to prepare labels with a piece of string attached to each. These were for the children who were soon to be deported.

In the early morning of July 16, between four and five o'clock, the raids began throughout Paris and its suburbs. A few lucky people who had been warned in time fled and joined the Resistance. Others committed suicide—106, according to Professor Abrami. Twenty-four sick and ailing, two of them women about to give birth, died during the raids.

A caravan of incongruous vehicles, fifty of them Paris buses that had been requisitioned for the purpose, transported men, women and children to the "primary centers"—the Vélodrome d'Hiver and a camp in Drancy. On July 16 and 17, a total of 12,884 people were arrested—3,031 men, 5,802 women, and 4,051 children.

All Jews who could do so crossed the demarcation line and sought refuge in the Unoccupied Zone. But they were scarcely more secure there as the raids and the arrests multiplied.

German pressure on the Vichy government had also increased in the area of labor recruitment. Laval was anxious to meet the German demands promptly, explaining that it was necessary "to avoid a forcible recruitment of personnel." But in actuality, his attitude signified a readiness to have the French themselves do what the enemy was not yet in a position to do.

On July 31, 40,000 workers, 10,000 of them skilled, left for

Germany. The freeing of French war prisoners in Germany had been used as a pretext; a mere 1,300 were sent home on August 11. But that didn't stop the Laval government from requisitioning additional workers.

The Resistance movement received a severe blow on September 25, when 280 S.D. and Gestapo agents, all of them carrying French police credentials, began to roam the Unoccupied Zone. They had at their disposal listening posts, direction-finding wireless equipment, and numerous vehicles, and they soon uncovered many of the clandestine radio transmitting sets around Lyon, Marseilles, Toulouse, and Pau. Most of the radio operators were arrested. At the same time, the Germans seized 20,000 weapons, large supplies of ammunition, and a good deal of cash.

Against the background of these traumatic events, Jean Moulin had proceeded with the creation of a new organizational framework for the Resistance. Moulin proposed to the various Resistance leaders that an officer of the Free French B.C.R.A. (Central Information and Action Bureau—*Bureau Central de Renseignements et d'Action*) be put in charge of preparing all future operations. Each Resistance group or movement would be responsible for finding proper airfields and supplying reception committees for the men who were dropped. An Aerial and Maritime Operation Service (*Services d'Opération Aériennes et Maritimes*), better known as the S.O.A.M., was organized; later it became the Center for Parachuting and Landing Operations (*Centre d'Opérations de Parachutage et d'Aterrissage*)— the C.O.P.A. Its final incarnation was the Bureau of Air Operations (*Bureau d'Operations Aériennes*)—B.O.A. In August the S.O.A.M., which Moulin personally directed, was divided into three regions: Lyon, for *Combat;* Clermont-Ferrand, for *Liberation*; and Toulouse for *Francs-Tireurs*. The head of each regional S.O.A.M. had his own radio receiving and transmitting set.

At the same time, Moulin began establishing agencies in the "civil" domain which the various Resistance movements could share. He advised the B.C.R.A. in April that he had set up an information and propaganda service (B.I.P.) "outside the Resistance movements but in harmony with them." The aims of the B.I.P. were to disseminate Allied information and propaganda throughout France; to spread the propaganda of the F.F.I. (*Force Françaises de l'Intérieur*) so that the Allies would be better informed about the activities of the Resistance; to transmit current news; and to prepare articles and documents to be published in the F.F.I., British, American, and neutral press.

Georges Bidault was chosen to direct this service. The B.I.P. bulletin made its debut in May 1942. At first it appeared monthly, then weekly, and later three times a week.

At de Gaulle headquarters and in France, complex political questions, anticipating the future, were being given increasing attention. In a letter dated June 23, Moulin recounted the conversations he had had in Toulouse regarding the formation of a political, administrative and economic body that would direct an examination "of official agencies to be either suppressed or created when the proper time came, and of groups holding important political, administrative or economic posts that ought to be eliminated. A suggested list of candidates for national and local posts would be presented in London when the examination had been completed."

This marked the beginning of the purge of collaborationists. The major statement issued by General de Gaulle on June 24 was quite clear on this point:

> The last veils under which the enemy and treachery have operated against France have now been destroyed. The stake in the war is clear to all Frenchmen: independence or slavery. It is the sacred duty of each of us to do everything possible to contribute to the liberation of our country from the heel of the oppressor. There is no future, no outcome but victory.

And he went on:

> But this gigantic ordeal has revealed to the nation that the danger which threatens its existence does not come solely from without, that a victory which fails to bring about a bold and

internal renovation will be no victory at all. A moral, social, political, economic regime abdicated in defeat, after having fallen into a paralyzing licentiousness. Another, the offspring of criminal capitulation, is infected with the poison of despotism. The French people condemn both of them. As they unite for victory, they look forward to revolution. . . .

On July 14 Free France changed its name to Fighting France (*La France Combattante*). The purpose was to demonstrate the solidarity of the Resistance within and outside the country.

Having overcome a thousand difficulties and rid the Resistance of countless intrigues, Jean Moulin achieved another important success: the creation of a coordinating committee that included the heads of the three main Resistance movements (or their deputies), plus the head of the Secret Army in the Occupied Zone. In a directive drafted on October 2, the committee's task was defined as follows:

It will coordinate all the activities of the three Resistance movements and see to it that responsibilities are evenly shared. The committee will present political suggestions to the National Committee, and it will implement, after due consultation, directives it receives from the National Committee. In regard to all military matters, the coordinating committee will take orders from General de Gaulle within the framework of the interallied strategic plan. The decisions reached by the coordinating committee will be carried out in part by the Resistance movements on instructions from their leaders, in part by the head of the Secret Army.

An important point was included:

It is clearly necessary to coordinate the paramilitary activities of the Resistance. The three movements will turn over their paramilitary groups to the Secret Army. Certain upper echelons may be recruited outside the movements themselves, with a part of the military staff being provided by the F.F.I. The head of the Secret Army in the Unoccupied Zone will be appointed by General de Gaulle.

General Delestraint was given command of the Secret Army in the Occupied Zone. Several rather sizable paramilitary troops had been organized during the past few months, including the *Francs-Tireurs et Partisans*, which drew its members from Lyon, the Rhône valley, and parts of the Massif Central.

The Communists, meanwhile, had formed a National Military Committee of their own. From the outset they sought to collect arms, recruit fighting formations, and launch military action.

The extreme German and Vichy pressure exerted on French workers resulted in a spontaneous strike on October 17. It began in Oullins, a suburb of Lyon. Within forty-eight hours, 13,000 workers had walked off their jobs. At a meeting of Resistance representatives and factory delegates in Lyon, a ringing proclamation was issued:

> In agreement with the National Committee of Fighting France, in agreement with General de Gaulle, the Resistance movements have achieved unification. They urge you:
>
> To sabotage all transport to Germany!
>
> To stage strikes in order to protect those workers who have refused to leave for Germany!
>
> To demand the release of all prisoners of war!

The proclamation was signed: *"Liberation, Combat, Francs-Tireurs, National Front, French Workers' Movement, French Communist Party."*

One hundred rebels were arrested at Oullins, but they were released the following day, and the lists of workers to be deported to Germany were removed from the factories. This success led to the establishment of strike committees in most of the cities of the southern zone. Jean Moulin, newly arrived in Lyon, provided subsidies for these committees.

During the closing days of 1942, the Germans, aided by blind or servile Frenchmen, pursued both Jews and Communists. Determined to obtain qualified workers for their factories beyond the Rhine, the Germans increasingly resorted to forcible recruitment. Threats hung in the air, each day affecting more and more people. The inevitable result was that a majority of the population came to be drawn into clandestine activity.

In other respects, Germany's situation was far from flourishing. German soldiers were bogged down in Russia, where they faced an imminent and bloody defeat at Stalingrad. The Balkans were in revolt. Surprise raids on Dieppe and St.-Nazaire gave the impression that large-scale operations impended on the western front. The American war machine, which had begun to function in December 1941, was now operating at full capacity. The Allies gave proof of their prowess with the North African landings in November. All these events sufficed to swing toward the Allied cause those Frenchmen who until now had been skeptical.

CHAPTER FIVE

~~~~~~~~

DISARRAY
AND UNITY

A T THE END of 1942, France was fragmented both politically and socially. The authority of the state was divided. First there was Marshal Pétain, who in 1940 was given full legal powers by a huge parliamentary majority—powers, however, that were purely theoretical. Pierre Laval, whose government was wholly dependent on the good will of the Germans, wielded whatever actual power his masters would allow.

Then there was Free France, whose leader, General de Gaulle, also claimed to be the embodiment of French legitimacy. He ruled over less than half of the French colonial empire and had at his disposal a courageous but not numerous phalanx whose means of existence were parsimoniously guaranteed by the Allies.

There was also the Imperial Council in Algiers, established by Admiral Darlan and presided over by him for three weeks— that is to say, until he was assassinated, on Christmas Eve, under troubled and troubling circumstances.

In addition, there were the Communists, who daily called for more and more direct action in their eagerness to make things easier for the embattled Soviet Union and to create a situation conducive to social revolution.

And finally there were the French masses, for whom everyday life was becoming increasingly difficult, oppressed as they were by tyranny, torn by conflicting propaganda, and suffering from a scarcity of food in most of their cities.

One of the major continuing concerns in France was how to contend with Germany's demand for labor. A large number of foreign skilled workers had to be recruited by Germany, whose armies were facing destruction on the eastern front. It was this problem that Gauleiter Sauckel discussed on February 11, 1943, at a meeting in the Paris headquarters of the Wehrmacht:

"The armaments industry must deliver by mid-March 200,-000 technicians. I have received an order from the Führer stating that these men must be replaced by 200,000 foreign skilled workers. I will need 150,000 technicians from France and 50,000 from Holland, Belgium and other countries. In addition, the Reich will require 100,000 unskilled workers from France.

"The French government is made up exclusively of experts in the art of stalling. Had the first 250,000 workers arrived in time in Germany, had they come in the autumn—remember, negotiations with the French government had begun as early as the preceding spring—we could have mobilized our technicians earlier and organized fresh army divisions. And then Stalingrad would not have been encircled. Be that as it may, the Führer is now absolutely determined to rule France, even without the help of the French government."

There was something comical about this view of the Vichy as an auxiliary of the Soviet Union![1]

---

1. Much later, Pierre Laval's lawyers were to use this argument in defense of their client.

Nevertheless, because of Gauleiter Sauckel's insistence, the Vichy government established the Service for Obligatory Labor (S.T.O.) on February 1. Young people born between 1920 and 1922 were to be recruited for work in German factories. From April to October, about 100,000 were thus "mobilized."

On February 23 all the prefects in the southern zone were called to Vichy by Laval. He instructed them to spur departures for Germany, using as bait the "release" of French prisoners. Young students were to finish out the school year before becoming eligible for deportation to Germany or for work in the factories. Under no circumstances could repatriated prisoners be sent to work in the factories of the Reich.

This was the period when Laval believed that the reversals on the eastern front, plus the increasing threat of Communism, would profoundly affect all aspects of the war and bring about a rapprochement between the British and Americans and the Germans. Whatever private reservations he may have had, and despite the shrewdness or cunning so often evident in his negotiations with the invaders, the public image projected by Pierre Laval was that of an ardent defender of collaboration, of a functionary automatically carrying out German decisions. Who could have realized at the time that his schemes and maneuvers, his lengthy discussions with the Germans, were not only useful but often necessary? His artful bargaining could hardly have been properly assessed by anyone outside his immediate entourage.

On the other hand, in the official domain, the head of the Vichy government dragged people with him along the road to an active collaboration that many Frenchmen, because of his assurances, were to practice in good faith. It is from this point of view that Laval's actions may be considered most blameworthy as well as most dangerous.

As early as June 22, 1942, Laval had declared in a radio address: "I am hoping for a German victory, because otherwise Bolshevism will spread everywhere. . . . France cannot remain passive and indifferent in view of the enormous sacrifices Germany is making in order to build a Europe in which we shall have our place . . ."

On December 13, 1942, he told the press in Vichy: "An American victory would be a triumph for the Jews and the Communists. As for myself, I have chosen . . ."

On January 30, 1943, when the guard units were converted into the "French militia" under Joseph Darnand's command, Laval said to them: "You are only a minority, but I prefer quality to quantity. . . . I would like the bond between you and me to be a close one. You shall be my companions." The misdeeds committed by this militia became notorious, but Joseph Darnand was later appointed secretary-general for the maintenance of "law and order."

On June 5, 1943, in another radio speech, Laval said, "There are Frenchmen fighting in Russia. They volunteered to go there. They symbolize all that is finest in our military tradition, for they are defending the true interests of France. Their government congratulates them and thanks them. It not only hopes that others will follow their example; it asks them to do so."

In the last analysis, anti-Communism was the Vichy regime's most powerful weapon. This is clearly attested by Marshal Pétain's 1943 Christmas message: "Listen to a man who is here only because of you and who loves you like a father. Once again, I beg you to think first of all of the mortal danger that threatens our country should a hideous civil war break out, or should Communism and its pagan barbarity triumph."

The German invasion of the Unoccupied Zone in November 1942 destroyed the myth of Vichy's independence. Until then, the regime had had at its disposal, at least in theory if not in reality, the Armistice Army of 100,000 men. In the event of a resumption of hostilities, Vichy's general staff had plans for using several assembly points where the reservists of every military region could gather.

The army had scant equipment. On orders from General Weygand, the organization created to conceal war matériel

(C.D.M.) had hidden vehicles, cannon, pistols, automatic rifles, and assorted munitions, including 150,000 grenades. It even managed to manufacture a new and particularly effective type of anti-tank grenade. But German counterespionage, considerably aided by a flood of denunciations, mostly anonymous, reduced the C.D.M.'s efforts to zero. The statistics on this organization are tragic—3 men executed, 103 deported (49 of them never again saw France), 202 interned!

On November 10, 1942, the Armistice Army was ready for battle. The general staff ordered the troops to leave their barracks. Army headquarters were transferred from Vichy to a manor house in Rapine, near Lezoux. According to the "Giraud plan," the man who escaped from the Loewenstein fortress, General Giraud, was to take charge of a joint expedition involving North Africa and the south of France. Although the plan had been considered and rejected by the Allies, Vichy knew nothing about it and did not even know what had become of Giraud. Darlan was in Algiers; as for Laval, he was in Berlin for further negotiations.

At a meeting of the cabinet, General Bridoux, Vichy's Minister of War, inveighed against the "seditious officers" who were attempting to drag the army into a rebellion. He went so far as to threaten to attack the manor house in Rapine with units of the *Garde mobile*. He ordered the troops to return to their garrisons, and, in the absence of any countervailing instructions, the officers obeyed. Not, however, General de Lattre de Tassigny, who assumed command of the few remaining soldiers willing to continue the fight. Abandoned by everyone, de Lattre was soon arrested and imprisoned on orders from Vichy. He barely escaped execution at the hands of the enemy.

And so the Germans encountered no resistance when they invaded the Unoccupied Zone on November 11. Judging by their statements of intent, one might have had the impression that the time of fraternity had arrived. Hitler concluded a message to Marshal Pétain with these words: "Germany is therefore determined to defend, hopefully side by side with the soldiers of France, not only the frontiers of your country but also the frontiers of culture and civilization."

But two weeks later came the Toulon affair and the scuttling of the French fleet. At the same time, army barracks were invaded and French troops ignominiously ejected. The resistance of Vichy's army was about to assume a new guise.

In December, at Clermont-Ferrand, the Resistance Organization of the Army (O.R.A.) was launched, under the direction of General Frère,[2] aided by generals Revers, Verneau, and Olleris; colonels Descour, Zeller, Pommies; and others. Members of the Intelligence Service, now incorporated into the O.R.A., were to serve as liaison with *Combat*. Under the guise of a newly formed Civic Service, a youth organization established by General de la Porte du Theil became a training center for soldiers and noncommissioned officers.

General Giraud, whose presence had been so sorely missed at a decisive moment, had left metropolitan France for Gibraltar on board a British submarine during the night of November 5. The Americans were counting on him to straighten out the North African imbroglio, but they soon discovered that his influence did not extend beyond a small circle of friends.

Since Darlan, not Giraud, became the Allies' man, his assassination was an event of major importance. De Gaulle quickly made the most of it. On December 25, he cabled Giraud: ". . . the murder in Algiers is an omen and a warning. . . . The need to establish a national authority is now more urgent than ever." He suggested that Giraud meet him as soon as possible, either in Algeria or in Chad, to "study ways and means of uniting under a provisional central power all the forces in both metropolitan France and her overseas territories that are capable of joining in the struggle for the liberation and defense of France."

---

2. Generals Frère and Verneau were arrested shortly and deported. General Revers succeeded General Frère.

Giraud, appointed Darlan's successor, sent de Gaulle an evasive reply, but the two men got together at Casablanca during the Roosevelt-Churchill conference in January 1943. The communiqué they issued after their meeting affirmed their "complete agreement on the goals to be achieved, which included the liberation of France and the triumph of human liberties through a total defeat of the enemy."

Goals were no problem, but the same could not be said about the means. On June 3, 1943, in Algiers, the French Committee of National Liberation (C.F.L.N.) was proclaimed to be "the sole central government of France." De Gaulle and Giraud were to serve as co-presidents of the committee—an arrangement which proved to be of short duration, as de Gaulle quickly assumed control. Giraud was named commander-in-chief of the Free French armed forces, and on November 9 he gave up his C.F.L.N. presidency. He was removed entirely from the picture in April 1944, when he retired.

Within France itself, meanwhile, the Coordinating Committee created by Jean Moulin had become the Executive Committee or Directorate, still chaired by Moulin. The following men were named to key posts: Henri Frenay, commissioner for military affairs; d'Astier de la Vigerie, commissioner for political affairs; Lenoir, commissioner for intelligence, security, and material resources, with authority to control the radio facilities and the service for forged documents. General Delestraint, head of the Secret Army, was placed under the jurisdiction of the Directorate.

As the activities of the various Resistance movements expanded and as recruitment for the Secret Army proceeded, costs naturally increased. Jean Moulin, who was responsible for supplying the financial needs of all the organizations, disbursed 7,888,900 francs during one short interval alone: the period from December 17, 1942, to January 10, 1943. In March expenses increased to 18,500,000 francs; by April the figure had risen to nineteen million. Most of the money went to the Secret Army and to the three networks in the southern zone.

Since London knew far less about northern France than it did about the former Unoccupied Zone, Pierre Brossolette was sent over to do some reconnoitering. He parachuted on January 27, on the "Brumaire" mission, and was soon followed by Colonel Passy, accompanied by a young British officer, Yeo Thomas, on the "Arquebuse" mission. The assignments given both missions involved important new steps in the organization of the Resistance—and in the future of France.

The functions of the "Brumaire" mission were spelled out as follows: "1) to proceed in the Occupied Zone toward the strictest possible separation of everything to do with intelligence from civil and military action; 2) to compile an inventory of all forces that might conceivably play a role in the pre-liberation national uprising and that are presently active in the Resistance, in special groups like the O.C.M.,[3] and in various political, labor, or religious organizations. Arrangements should be made to place such forces at the disposal of the E.M.Z.O. . . ;[4] and 3) to seek out, through direct contact and cooperation with the abovementioned groups and organizations, those individuals who might staff the provisional bureaucracy when the day of liberation comes."

Passy, for his part, was responsible for making known throughout the Occupied Zone all of General de Gaulle's directives that had to do with both military and civil matters. In performing this function, with the cooperation of Moulin and the head of the "Brumaire" mission, he was: "A) to decide what measures to take, with an eye to rationalizing the operations of the various intelligence networks; B) to establish contact with all Resistance groups in the Occupied Zone in order to coordi-

---

3. *Organization Civile et Militaire,* the Civil and Military Organization. It not only was a Resistance group but also performed intelligence operations.

4. The general staff of the Occupied Zone. Under the direction of General Delestraint, it was the counterpart of the Secret Army in the Unoccupied Zone.

nate military operations within the Occupied Zone, and also to arrange for the two zones to coordinate their separate military operations; and C) to examine the conditions under which it will be possible to organize a Central Executive Committee empowered to settle all civil questions."

On March 20 the heads of the two missions sent an encouraging message to the B.C.R.A. in London: "A) Please inform the general that we have gotten the F.T.P. to place their people under the orders of the heads of regional subdivisions of the Secret Army. B) Beginning in April, all groups will furnish a full listing of the forces at their disposal in each of the departments, and in addition they will provide a schedule of the operations to be carried out during the ensuing month. C) Total military and civil cooperation has been established between all groups in the Occupied Zone."

Early in February, Passy's adjutant, Manuel, had reported after a tour of inspection in France that it was imperative to create a nationwide "executive committee" headed by Jean Moulin and embracing the representatives of Resistance movements, trade unions, and political parties in both the northern and the southern zones.

Moulin had recommended to General de Gaulle the creation of a National Council of the Resistance. René Mostache has detailed his reasons for doing so:[5]

> To provide a secure base for the activities of General de Gaulle; to bolster and legitimize his authority in the eyes of the Allies and the people of France; to eliminate ideological and personal conflicts and put an end to the rivalry that pitted movements against political parties and leaders of movements against delegates to the National Committee; to thwart the Giraudist and American attempt "to whitewash" Vichy as well as to foil

5. *Le Conseil National de la Résistance*. Presses Universitaires de France, 1958.

the Communist scheme to seize control of the entire internal Resistance; to avert all the risks of a split that might result from this and to achieve the definitive unification of the Resistance.

On February 21 the leader of Fighting France handed Moulin a directive making him "the sole representative of General de Gaulle and of the National Committee for all of metropolitan France." The general also laid down the following instructions:

There shall be created, as speedily as possible, a single Council of the Resistance for all of metropolitan France. Jean Moulin, representing General de Gaulle, is to chair it. This Council of the Resistance will guarantee representation for Resistance groups, resisting political parties and resisting trade unions. The projected coalition shall be effected on the basis of the following principles: enmity toward the Germans, their allies and accomplices, to be implemented by every available means, especially by the use of guns; struggle against all dictatorships and notably the Vichy regime, regardless of the kind of exterior with which it might adorn itself; promotion of freedom; alignment with de Gaulle in the fight which he is waging to liberate French territory and restore to the people of France their right to speak out. . . . In order to make sure that the Council of the Resistance will have the prestige and efficacy it requires, its members must be men who enjoy the confidence of the groups they represent and can issue commands without delay in the name of their constituents. The Council of the Resistance constitutes the embryo of a body representing the French nation on a reduced scale— the Political Council that will work with General de Gaulle when he returns to France. As soon as he again sets foot on French soil, the Council of the Resistance will be enlarged by the addition of supplementary delegates. . . . The representative of General de Gaulle, President of the Council of the Resistance, will serve as the regular intermediary between the Council of the Resistance on the one hand, and the general staff of the Army of the Interior, the Center for Research, and the Intelligence Service, on the other.

A few days before, de Gaulle had bestowed the Cross of Liberation on Jean Moulin. This very private ceremony occurred in the drawing room of de Gaulle's house in Hampstead outside London. Passy has described the occasion:

> I can still see Moulin, deathly pale, in the grip of an emotion that possessed us all. He was standing a few feet from de Gaulle as the general whispered to him: "Stand at attention." When de Gaulle continued, his words came in that staccato way he had of stressing each syllable, a manner of speaking that has since become familiar to all of us: "Corporal Mercier,[6] we recognize you as our Companion, for the Liberation of France, in all honor and for victory." And as de Gaulle embraced him, a large tear of gratitude, pride and fierce determination gently ran down the pale cheek of our comrade, Moulin. He looked up at de Gaulle, and we could see on his throat the scars of self-inflicted razor cuts dating from 1940, when he had courted death in order to resist yielding to Nazi torture.[7]

By the time Moulin again left for France on March 21 aboard the *Lysander,* accompanied by General Delestraint and Christian Pineau, he had become a member of the French National Committee. On March 30 he was in Paris, and there he encountered a difficult situation. Some 200 resisters, among them his aide, Manhès, had been arrested. All those who had escaped the German net had to go underground. This did nothing to simplify his task. On April 3 he chaired a meeting of representatives of the various Resistance movements in the northern zone. Acting in concert with the B.C.R.A., Delestraint had put the finishing touches to the military organization of the zone during his stay in London. Like the southern zone, the one in the north was divided into six regions.

---

6. This was the cover name that Moulin had adopted in London. Actually, he was a corporal in the reserves.

7. As a matter of fact, Moulin had slashed himself not with a razor but with a piece of glass.

The Allies' main concern at this time was to impede the arrival of German reinforcements at the moment of landings in western Europe and the concurrent opening of a second front. "We therefore had to cut railway lines, blow up bridges, disrupt the long-distance telephonic communications of German headquarters," Jacques Soustelle has related.

> These were the objectives of our sabotage plans, especially of the so-called "green plan." We had to determine which were the most important and vulnerable points on railways and highways; to ready the secret groups, arm them with weapons and above all with explosives, making sure they understood their assignments and were prepared to carry them out when the signal was given via a "personal message" over the BBC; to maintain these groups intact and hold them in reserve until D-day.

Very different attitudes were evident in regard to these plans. Allied military men, indifferent to the idea of arming a popular resistance, preferred to confine military action to the accomplishment of their own plans. They were content to have at their disposal small groups that would carry out specific assignments and that would hold on to their caches of equipment until the opportune moment. On the other hand, the Communists and the F.T.P. continued to want to take immediate action without being bound in any way by the general operations in progress.

"France was at war; she therefore had to fight," Jacques Soustelle wrote in *Envers et Contre Tout*.

> But it would have been absurd and criminal to make her fight in any chance place and in a haphazard way. Hence the idea of making a distinction between four very different kinds of action, each depending on its own personnel: first, missions that had already been arranged according to plan, with their sabotage groups; second, "immediate action," favored by those who wanted to strike at the enemy before D-day, to damage his mili-

tary and industrial potential, sabotage his transports and the factories that supplied him, and finally to keep alive among the armed elite in the Resistance the spirit of battle lest it gradually disintegrate. This required the formation of special units called *"groupes-francs"*; third, action by the Secret Army, which was to prepare and organize but not to intervene until D-day, when a general uprising could complete the rout of an already badly shaken enemy; last of all, action by the Maquis, whose existence was due to the establishment of the Service for Obligatory Labor (S.T.O.). The Maquis had to be armed and fed to make sure it could survive; then it was to do its share, together with the Secret Army, in liberating vast sections of the country.

It was the Germans' demand for labor, as Soustelle notes, that spurred the formation of the Maquis in the spring of 1943. Thus, in the region of Grenoble, for example, students threatened by the S.T.O. went up to la Villete de Vaujany, where Joseph Perrin ran a camp. They were soon joined by other recruits who spread out in sections of Bessey d'Oz and Villard-Notre-Dame. This was the beginning of the Maquis of Oisans. In the Ain, small groups of rebels appeared, and a school for cadres began to function in June at Gorges, near Mongriffon. In Haute-Savoie, Maquis groups appeared here and there under the leadership of Commander Vallette d'Osia. Another school for cadres was opened in Cluses as early as February. In Corrèze, by the summer of 1943, there were 1,000 Maquis. In the northern zone, the number of Maquis spurted when the class of 1942 was called up for forced labor in Germany. Groups usually consisting of about twenty men formed, especially in Brittany, northern Normandy, Burgundy, in the Aube and the Ardennes.

On April 12 an organizational meeting of the Secret Army was held in the northern zone. General Delestraint explained the directives worked out in London for the formation of a force that was to go into action on the day fixed by the Allies. All the paramilitary movements were asked to contribute to the Secret

Army. Pierre Villon, the representative of the Communist-controlled National Front, vehemently protested the London plan, saying he would never agree to interrupt "immediate action." Jean Moulin took a dim view of this and replied sharply.

Actually, of course, there was no question of abandoning the idea of immediate action. It was simply a matter of taking action that was compatible with the final goal, provided that such action was disciplined and coordinated.

That was the purpose of the "personal and secret instructions" which de Gaulle sent to General Delestraint on May 21, 1943. He stated explicitly that during the initial period "the principle of the need for immediate action will be acceptable." Such action would be spearheaded by small numbers of fighters grouped into *corps francs* and "professional cells." Delestraint was not to interfere in this domain unless he received very broad directives regarding the categories of objectives to be attacked, the areas that were to be the targets of immediate action, and the technical conditions under which a helping hand or sabotage might be possible. But Delestraint's essential mission prior to D-day was to ready the army inside the country so that it would be prepared to take part in the Allied military operations. On D-day, Delestraint was to assume effective command of the army of the interior and the *groupes francs*. He would be responsible for coordinating the insurrectional operations of the professional cells with the purely military action of the army of the interior.

The anarchical structure of the Maquis posed a grave problem. Like General de Gaulle, Jean Moulin felt that too much was being done in anticipation of events and that the Maquis ran the risk of not being able to hold out until the day of the Allied military landings. Furthermore, there was a political aspect to the problem. Moulin knew full well that the leaders of certain Resistance movements were using the Maquis to create a second secret army.

This was precisely what the Communists had in mind when

they refused to subscribe to the *attentisme* of London. Charles Tillon wrote:[8]

> The young rebels, burning to become Partisans, often clashed with the wait-and-see policy of the leaders who issued their orders from London. We could see these leaders trying to transform the Maquis into farmers (a few wealthy landowners were quick to take advantage of this illegal and undemanding work force).
>
> Often a local leader would house the young people in an abandoned farmhouse, do everything he could to keep them alive, but in bringing them food he would also transmit the B.C.R.A.'s paralyzing orders: do nothing, wait. Such directives went against the grain, offending the young rebels' pride, their eagerness for battle. . . .
>
> The young people solved the conflict in two ways: either by placing themselves under the jurisdiction of the F.T.P. if a "contact" made this possible; or by forcing their leaders (who themselves often preached *attentisme* reluctantly, out of a fierce sense of loyalty to their superiors) to take action or at least to authorize them to do so.

On May 27, 1943, the C.N.R. (National Council of the Resistance) met for the first time in Corbin's Paris apartment, 48 Rue du Four. Moulin presided. The five movements in the Occupied or northern zone were represented by Madelin (*Ceux de la Libération*), Lecompte-Boinet (*Ceux de la Résistance*), Pierre Villon (*Front National*), Charles Laurent (*Liberátion Nord*), and Sermoy (*O.C.M.*). Claude Bourdet (*Combat*), Pascal Copeau (*Libération*), and Antoine Avinin (*Francs-Tireurs*) represented the three Resistance movements in the Unoccupied or southern zone. Political parties were represented by André Mercier (Communist), André le Troquer (Socialist), Marc Rucart (Radical), Georges Bidault (Christian Democrat), Jacques Debû-Bridel (Republican Federation), and Jo-

---

8. *Les F.T.P.,* Juilliard, 1962.

seph Laniel (Democratic Alliance). For the trade unions there were Louis Saillant of the C.G.T. and Gaston Tessier of the C.F.T.C.

In his opening statement, Jean Moulin issued a warning: "The presence of representatives of former political parties should not be viewed as official approval of the restoration of these parties in the form in which they functioned prior to the Armistice. I have insisted upon the very opposite in order to insure that the necessary intellectual and disciplined effort will be made to establish large ideological groups capable of giving stability to French public life."

Then Moulin read General de Gaulle's message to the C.N.R.[9] Stressing "unity of action," the leader of Free France declared, "If the liberation and the victory are to be truly French, it is imperative and necessary for the nation to unite in a purely French effort. Our immediate interests, our future greatness, perhaps our very independence, are at stake. Anything that makes for dispersion, isolated action, special alliances in any domain of the overall struggle, compromises both the force of the blows dealt the enemy by France and her own national cohesion.

"The present war is a colossal revolution for all nations, but above all for France. It is therefore supremely imperative that the nation should act in such a way as to emerge from liberation in an orderly and independent fashion. This means that the nation must be organized in advance so that it can be governed and administered without undue delay, in accordance with what France herself desires. She can then await the time when she will be able to express herself normally through a vote of all her citizens."

Georges Bidault, in agreement with Jean Moulin, offered a motion that was unanimously adopted after a brief but lively

---

9. This message is dated May 10, 1943.

discussion. A massive vote of confidence in de Gaulle, as he was about to go to Algiers, the text read:

The National Council of the Resistance enthusiastically welcomes the decision of General de Gaulle and General Giraud reached on the morrow of this victory, to meet shortly in Algiers in order to achieve the unity of all French forces combating the enemy of the nation and his accomplices within the country.

France, already represented on all fronts, wishes to enter this liberating war even more forcefully and to donate all the resources of her liberated Empire. To achieve this end fully, she must as soon as possible have a single strong government that can coordinate and lead, thereby affirming to the world that France has recovered her prestige as a great nation.

France expects this government—it is the duty of this Council to declare this quite clearly—to be entrusted to General de Gaulle, who was the soul of the Resistance during the somber days of the struggle and who, ever since June 18, 1940, has labored incessantly, with complete lucidity and total independence, to prepare the way for the rebirth of our devastated country and the restoration of our mangled republican liberties.

France ardently desires to see General Giraud, who together with the Allies has paved the way for and insured the victory in North Africa, assume command of the revivified French Army.

In his report of June 4 to de Gaulle, Jean Moulin observed: "I am pleased to be able to inform you that not only did all the members attend the meeting but that the meeting itself proceeded in an atmosphere of patriotic unity and dignity that I feel called upon to underscore."

But he also noted: "I won't mention the material difficulties of organizing a meeting of seventeen members, all of them sought, or at any rate watched, by the police and the Gestapo." For security reasons, the C.N.R. held no more plenary sessions until the liberation.

Although Jean Moulin was extremely cautious, he could feel that the net was closing in around him. In a report dated May 7, he noted that a circular of the *Mouvements Unis de Résistance,* the umbrella organization better known as the M.U.R., had fallen into the hands of the Gestapo three days after it had been distributed. He went on to say, "In this circular, all my activities for the last eighteen months were outlined and explained, and the way I had been moving about was noted. The text also sketched some of General Delestraint's activities.

"The Vichy police and the Gestapo are fully informed about my identity and my actions. My task is therefore becoming more and more delicate at a time when the difficulties surrounding me are forever increasing. I'm determined to hold out as long as possible, but should I disappear, I would not have had time enough to brief my successors."

The Gestapo, now in complete charge throughout France, was aided and abetted by Frenchmen belonging to Darnand's militia. There were paid informers, but also some who volunteered their help—people who believed in Hitler's Great Europe and others who acted from personal spite or simple stupidity. Political hatred also played a role and would continue to do so in both camps. Most important, the Germans were very well informed about the development of the Secret Army.

As early as March 1943, as Jean Moulin was to learn, the Gestapo in Marseille, headed by S.S. officer Dunker (known also as Delage), had seized a letter drop used by the M.U.R. As a result of this discovery, the Germans cast a net, bagging twenty people, among them Colonel Duboin, the regional head of the Secret Army. Those arrested also included Multon (alias Lunel), who agreed to work for the Gestapo. Through a meeting arranged by Multon, Berthy Albrecht, Frenay's collaborator, was arrested at Macon. Condemned to death, the poor woman was decapitated with an axe.

On June 8 at Châlon-sur-Saône, Multon and a German

named Moog arrested René Hardy (alias Didot), head of the railway sabotage service. Didot had a date to meet General Delestraint the next morning at nine o'clock in the Muette Metro station. It was Moog who presented himself to Delestraint with these words:[10] "My general, I have come at the request of Didot. He thinks that the Muette Metro station is an unhealthy place to meet. He wants you to join him at the Passy Metro station instead. He is waiting there for you."

Delestraint followed Moog and got into his car. He soon found himself at Gestapo headquarters on Avenue Foch.

Three-quarters of an hour later, Colonel Gastaldo, head of the Secret Army's *deuxième bureau,* and Lieutenant Theobald, who were waiting for the general at the Pompe Métro station, were also arrested.

Meanwhile, the Gestapo released Hardy, undoubtedly hoping that he would lead them to the principal leaders of the French Resistance. And they figured correctly. It was through René Hardy that Barbié, the head of the Lyon Gestapo, managed to discover that a meeting was scheduled in Dr. Dugoujon's house in Caluie for June 21. And yet the rendezvous had been planned with the utmost discretion.

The doctor's villa, with its ivy-colored walls and its little garden, was located in a quiet neighborhood. The waiting room was filled with patients, including several resisters. What could be more natural?

A few cars stopped in front of the house, Place Castellane. "German police," the men inside the vehicles called to the doctor as he saw a patient out the door.

Did they know that Jean Moulin was among the men they captured at the doctor's? Apparently it took the Gestapo a few days to identify him. In any event, only one man managed to

---

10. It has been established that the Gestapo knew about the planned meeting before Hardy's arrest.

escape at that time: René Hardy. Arrested once again on the following day, Hardy took advantage of a favorable opportunity and again escaped.[11]

Christian Pineau, recently arrested by the Gestapo, was interned at the Montluc fortress. There, among the new arrivals walking in the courtyard during the recreation hour, he spotted Jean Moulin. He wrote:[12]

> Moulin's arrest was a catastrophe for the Resistance. No one for a single instant doubted the man's courage. He would never talk, no matter what they did to him. But he held in his hands so many strands that it would be extremely difficult to unravel them. Should the landings take place in the autumn, all the preparations on French soil would suffer an appreciable delay.

On June 24 a curious thing happened to Pineau. He was taken from his cell at six o'clock in the evening and taken before a German noncommissioned officer, who said, "Don't get dressed, Monsieur, and take your razor." He has described what happened next:

> Why this strange order? I went downstairs; no sentries carrying machine guns accompanied us. Nothing stirred in the prison. The noncommissioned officer took me out into the northern section of the courtyard and led me to a bench where a man lay stretched out, guarded by a soldier with a gun strapped to his shoulder.
> "Shave, Monsieur."
> To my stupefaction and horror I realized that the man lying there was none other than Jean Moulin. He was unconscious, his eyes sunken as if they had been pushed back into his head. On his temple was an ugly bluish wound. A slight rattling sound escaped

---

11. René Hardy stood trial after the liberation. Twice he was acquitted: in 1947 by a civil court and in 1950 by a military tribunal.
12. *La Résistance*, Juilliard, 1960.

from his swollen lips. It was obvious that he had been tortured by the Gestapo.

My hands trembling, I finished shaving while the soldier looked on as indifferent as if he were waiting his turn in a barber shop. Minutes passed.

Suddenly Moulin opened his eyes. He looked at me. I was certain he had recognized me, but what was he to make of my presence at his side at this moment?

"Drink," he murmured.

I turned to the soldiers. *"Ein wenig wasser."*

There was a second's hesitation; then one of the soldiers took a quart bottle filled with soapy water, rinsed it out at the water fountain, and brought it back full of fresh water.

Meanwhile I was leaning over Moulin, whispering a few stupid, trite, comforting phrases. He uttered five or six words in English which I couldn't understand because his voice was so cracked, his delivery so halting. He drank a little water from the bottle I handed him, then again lost consciousness.

Exhausted by the torture inflicted on him, Jean Moulin died on July 11 while being transferred to Germany. He had not talked.

Thus the French Resistance lost its finest hero, with the most serious consequences.

As early as July 27, Claude Serreulles, Moulin's adjutant, alluded in a report to "the fierce quarrels on the regional level that often pit the leaders of rival (but supposedly united) movements against one another." The Communist Party, which, under various guises, became the largest and most powerful group because it was the best structured, was to benefit from this new anarchical situation. The internal Resistance was to be more and more affected by the revolutionary war aims of the Communist Party.

CHAPTER SIX

~~~~~~~~

CORSICA,
FIRST
TO BE FREE

T HE ISLAND OF Corsica supplied the French Resistance with the word *maquis*—originally the name of the wild Corsican brush country, a natural hiding place for outlaws. And in the annals of the Resistance, Corsica holds the special place of first French department to be liberated.

As early as April 1941, Fred Scamaroni, an F.F.I. fighter, was sent to Corsica by the B.C.R.A. to organize the Resistance movement there. In July 1941, atfer the German invasion of Russia, the Communist Party, under the leadership of Arthur Giovani, had created a Corsican National Front. Proceeding very skillfully, the party was careful to stress the patriotic character of the organization. There was only one non-Communist among its leaders, Henri Maillot, but the fact that he was a relative of General de Gaulle sufficed to assure a much-needed liaison with the *Franc-Tireur* movement in Lyon. Giovani, for his part, established contact with the *Libération* group in Marseille.

A small Italian presence on Corsica was greatly enlarged on November 11, 1942, when an Italian fleet appeared at Bastia. Believing that the Allies were arriving to liberate them, a joyous crowd of people rushed to the port. Their disappointment was keen.

Within the next few days, the Italian occupation reached sizable proportions: 100,000 men in a population of less than 200,000. And this occupation was especially severe because it was supervised by the Fascist secret police—the O.V.R.A.—which emulated the Gestapo.

Maritime traffic, suspended since November 21, was resumed on December 2, but the Allies were sinking cargo ships, and the supply situation in Corsica grew increasingly difficult. A report dated June 1, 1943, was quite explicit: "No meat, fish, or vegetables; bread is rationed at 125 grams per day, and the people subsist primarily on sweet chestnut flour. The occupying forces seize everything. . . . Corsica is totally dependent on the outside world for its food, raw materials and manufactured products."

At the end of November 1942, the submarine *Casabianca,* one of the few warships that escaped scuttling in Toulon, arrived in Algiers, and its commander, Captain l'Herminier, was ordered to contact French Intelligence. Preparations were being made for an operation christened "Pearl Harbor" which was to bring Allied intelligence agents to Corsica. Commander de Saule, of the Air Force's Intelligence Service, headed the mission, accompanied by an American O.S.S. agent, two French noncommissioned officers, and a radio quartermaster.

The *Casabianca* got under way during the evening of December 11. On the fourteenth, it spent the day submerged near the Corsican coast. At a little past midnight on December 15, the crew was ordered to their battle stations. Silently, the submarine surfaced, heading cautiously for the Bay of Chioni. L'Herminier noted:[1]

---

1. *Casabianca,* Editions France-Empire.

Accustomed as we were to the darkness, we gradually discerned the outlines of the bay. It was then that we became aware of how close to land we were. The realization was both reassuring and agonizing: it would be quite easy to trap us offshore. But having penetrated this far into enemy territory, we felt we had forced an entry into the island and that we no longer ran any risk.

Meanwhile, the landing site was right there in front of us. The silence was total. Our electric propellers were set at low speed and made no sound. Although we had been submerged for twenty-four hours and confined inside the submarine, we didn't dare to turn on the fresh air ventilators and the exhaust fans. Both make quite a bit of noise on this type of ship. We were gliding in gently, and the cliffs straight ahead seemed to grow taller and taller.

A dinghy was put into the water, and the landing party reached the shore without mishap.

On February 5, 1943, the *Casabianca* arrived in the Bay of Arone with its first batch of munitions: 450 Sten guns and 60,000 rounds of ammunition.

Until munitions could be flown in, the *Casabianca* remained the best and most reliable means of transport. On July 3 the submarine unloaded thirteen tons of munitions on the Saleccia beach at the edge of the Agriates desert. On July 31 and August 1, twenty tons of weapons and other munitions were again deposited at the same spot after a close call in the Gulf of Porto, where the *Casabianca* had been subjected to heavy fire.

The Italians did not sit idly by. After someone denounced Fred Scamaroni, his radio communications were intercepted, and the O.V.R.A. agents began their manhunt. They found Scamaroni and tortured him, but he refused to talk, preferring suicide. The Italian police were left with no clue as to his true identity, and for the moment the Corsican Resistance was saved from disaster. But another net was cast, and this time the F.F.I. organization was completely dismantled, temporarily leaving the field open to the Communists' National Front.

On April 1, 1943, a British submarine landed Commander Colonna d'Istria, called Césari, on Corsica's eastern coast. General Giraud had commissioned Césari to coordinate the activities of all the local Resistance movements. It was he who was to take over the work interrupted after Scamaroni's death.

For four months Césari canvassed the Maquis. From a network consisting of 2,000 members he had to create a truly national secret army. In addition, landing fields for parachute drops had to be found, and the objectives of D-day clearly defined.

In an interview with André Maurois, Césari, a lively and very likable man, described his activities:[2]

"The dynamo of the movement? No, it didn't need a dynamo. Don't write that I was 'the soul of the Resistance'; every man gave his heart and soul to it. My job was to arm the fighters, to give them a framework of sorts, and above all to prevent them from taking off too soon, from getting themselves killed to no purpose.

"One night, loaded down with equipment, I was landed by submarine on a Corsican beach. The patriots who were supposed to be waiting there for me weren't there. With the help of the sailors, I had to unload and conceal the weapons, then get to a village and arrange for their transport. Many of our men no longer had shoes. They had to carry heavy loads through the underbrush, where needlelike growths tore the skin on their bare feet. Some of my friends were shot and their weapons seized. I myself was surrounded by the enemy in a grotto that fortunately for me had a passage to another grotto. They didn't know about this. When they tossed their grenades in, I was no longer there. . . . They set fires in five different places, hoping to capture me, but I had faithful shepherds who knew every road."

The first parachute drop, in May 1943, was marred by an accident. A container full of explosives slipped out of the para-

---

2. Quoted by André Maurois in *Miroir de l'Histoire*.

chute and exploded in the middle of the night. And the parachute itself, suddenly relieved of its burden, was carried away
by the wind and came down in enemy territory. But the Italians
searched in vain for the four tons of matériel that were dropped
without mishap.

The bloodletting increased. On June 17 in Ajaccio, two
members of the Maquis, Giusti and Mondolini, in the café "La
Brasserie Nouvelle," were attacked by carabinieri. Having no
illusions about their chances for survival, the two men decided
to make the Italians pay dearly for their lives. They were killed,
but not before killing eleven carabinieri. Then the Italians lost
their heads. Machine guns strafed the streets, firing at random.
A trawler lying at anchor in the port opened fire, as if the city
were staging an insurrection.

In the month of August, Césari's headquarters were surrounded by 1,200 armed men and set on fire. But to no avail.
Césari and his companions managed to escape. They continued
to carry out their mission of receiving and distributing weapons
and other munitions.

Césari was a man of remarkable aplomb. Admiral Lepotier
relates the following story:[3]

> To meet the demands of the French Intelligence Service,
> Colonna—whose official duties were limited solely to actual
> combat—set up an intelligence network. To insure its success,
> he enrolled himself in the enemy's service. In his pocket there
> was a membership card to prove it.
>
> One evening when he was in Bastia preparing to receive a
> cargo of munitions in the very heart of the city, he was arrested.
> He refused to allow himself to be searched. Even though tommy
> guns were leveled at him, he imposed his will on the carabinieri,
> finally persuading them to take him to General Stivale, the com-
> mander. Very confidentially, he showed the general an order in-
> dicating that he was on the side of the invader. He was not only

---

3. *Cap sur la Corse,* Editions France-Empire.

instantly released but also showered with embarrassed apologies. An enemy car was placed at his disposal. Thanks to it, that very night five tons of munitions earmarked for the patriots entered Bastia. The Italian chauffeur, who was drunk, was not aware of anything unusual. And that was just as well for him.

The march of events in Italy profoundly affected the situation in Corsica. On July 10, 1943, the Allies landed in Sicily, and just two months later, on September 8, Italy's surrender was announced.

News of the surrender reached Ajaccio on the evening of September 8. The leaders of the National Front, meeting in an olive grove in Casona, at the gates of the city, decided to spur an uprising.

After a few emissaries had been dispatched, a thousand young people rushed into the streets of Ajaccio, heading for the prefecture. The prefect refused to see them, and they retreated, but only to strike more effectively. The departmental committee of the National Front set itself up as a prefectural council and occupied the city on the following day.

Césari realized that it would be impossible to restrain this popular movement. He knew too that the Allies, whose prime objective at the moment was continental Italy, were not burning to liberate Corsica. General Giraud had warned the Corsicans: "Please tell the patriots that I am counting on them not to act prematurely."

With all this in mind, Césari hastened to address himself to General Magli, commander of the four Italian divisions stationed in the central and western sections of the island: "Let me know unequivocally before midnight tonight whether you are with us, against us, or neutral."

"With you," Magli immediately replied.

On the German side, twin tasks of directing the evacuation of Sardinia and defending Corsica were entrusted to General von Senger und Etterlin. Opposed by the Italians and the

French resisters, he could count only on the S.S. "Reichsführer" brigade stationed at Bonifaccio and Porto-Vecchio. In Bastia, Senger had only one infantry battalion and three heavy-artillery batteries, plus some naval and air units. The air force at his disposal, in fact, was far from negligible and could if necessary be reinforced by planes from France and Italy.

But the German general's forces were not sufficient to disarm the Italian troops. Moreover, General Magli, resorting to the kind of double game played by so many others, hastened to offer all possible support to the German command—to help in the evacuation of German troops from Sardinia and also to put an end to the resistance of French armed bands. Meanwhile, Césari had intervened.

On the evening of September 8, the small German garrison in Bastia attacked the port and the Italian vessels tied up there, but the operation proved a fiasco. The next day, a column of German soldiers could be seen trudging along, disarmed and surrounded by gun-toting Italians. Senger felt it was indispensable to recapture Bastia and attempted to negotiate with Magli. Their discussions dragged on for four days, and during the night of September 13–14, the Germans seized the port and occupied virtually the entire western coast of Corsica. Despite the resistance put up by the Italian forces and the harassing tactics of the Corsican patriots, German communications with the Continent were from then on assured.

On September 9, at six in the evening, General Giraud had received a message from Césari:

"Insurgents masters of Ajaccio. Italians passive. Fighting in Bastia. Corsica requests army's help."

Giraud immediately asked the Allies for ships. He was turned down because at that moment all Allied resources were committed to the Italian campaign. The next day, he summoned the heads of his General Staff, General Leyer for the army, General Bouscat for the air force, and Admiral Lemonnier for the navy, along with René Mayer, commissioner for the merchant marine, to compile an inventory of available forces. Troops could be found, but means of transport were lacking. Admiral Lemonnier emphasized the risk involved. Their only chance was to effect a surprise landing of 500 shock troops and take quick possession of the port. At the time there were only five French warships in the Mediterranean: three submarines—the *Casabianca,* the *Aréthuse,* and the *Perle*—and two light cruisers —the *Fantasque* and the *Terrible.* In order to use them, France had to get the consent of Admiral Andrew Cunningham, Allied commander-in-chief in the Mediterranean, who was in Salerno. At 6:00 A.M. on September 11, Cunningham gave the green light.

A second cable from Césari arrived in Algiers: "Patriots control prefecture and all administrative services. Pact with Italians against Germans. Allies awaited. Order prevails. Germans at Bastia, with Chiobini and Lioghi, are already isolated by Italian troops but danger remains imminent. Arrive via Ajaccio without danger. Ask for a pilot to direct you. We have a ship."

Giraud summoned General Henry Martin and said to him: "I've arrived at a decision: we must go to Corsica. The patriots, whom we've been arming for the past several months, have revolted. They're asking for help. Many people here regard their action as premature. The Germans continue to hold Sardinia. They have from 10,000 to 15,000 men with tanks in Corsica. But the signing of an armistice by the Italians has dealt them a blow. If we allow them to recoup, our Corsican compatriots may suffer terrible reprisals, and we will have lost a chance that will not soon recur."

Giraud put General Martin in charge of the operation, which was promptly christened "Vesuvius." To carry it out, Martin would have at his disposal Group Number 2, which included the shock battalion, to be landed on the island without delay; the Fourth Moroccan Alpine Division; a group of Moroccan cavalrymen; some men from the general reserves; and a few units attached to Base 901. The initial assignment was to establish a sizable bridgehead around Ajaccio in order to facilitate the landing of the bulk of the forces required for the conquest of the island.

At the same time, Admiral Lemonnier assembled the French and British officers who would be in charge of the troop transport ships. These men learned that the *Fantasque* and the *Terrible,* which were involved in the Salerno operations, would return to Algiers on the following day; that the torpedo-boat *Tempête,* recalled to Casablanca, would arrive at the same time; that it would be followed by another torpedo-boat, *Alcyon,* and then by the cruiser *Jeanne d'Arc* (now on its way from the Antilles). As for the crusier *Montcalm,* it would sail from Dakar. The R.A.F. could not provide air cover because Ajaccio was too far from its Sicilian bases.

Captain l'Herminier of the *Casabianca* was seated "in the last row of this brilliant gathering." He later recalled:

"The admiral looked at me. He was probably thinking that although the *Casabianca* was a very small vessel, nothing should be overlooked."

Lemonnier asked: "L'Herminier, how many members of the shock battalion would you be able to transport to Corsica without delay?"

"A hundred, Admiral, plus a forty-eight-hour supply of combat equipment," l'Herminier replied.

Captain Fawks, commander of the Eighth British Submarine Fleet, to which French submarines were attached for operational purposes, expressed his surprise. "Your commander is exaggerating a little, Admiral. That's impossible on a 1,500-ton submarine."

But in fact, l'Herminier knew exactly what he was talking about, having made an experiment of this kind less than two weeks before.

"When can you leave?" Lemonnier asked.

"In two and a half hours, Admiral."

The shock battalion, billeted at Staoueli, twelve miles from

Algiers, was ready to go. At 6:00 P.M. on September 11, the *Casabianca* set off for the bay at Lava, in Corsica. On board were 109 members of the shock battalion (three of them "clandestine" fighters who had managed to slip in at the last moment) and a crew reduced to a minimum of sixty-one men (out of eighty-five). That made a total of 170 men in all!

Cruising at seventeen knots, the submarine could surface because enemy forces were concentrating on Italy. Apropos of this, l'Herminier later recalled:

> In any case, I would have continued to surface in order not to lose time, for the small fry aboard were not eager to prolong their stay in what seemed to them to resemble the Métro during the rush hours.
>
> Our fighters resigned themselves to discomfort; they'd been uncomfortable before. But what really irked them was the thought that their pals would set foot on French soil after having sailed about like millionaire yachtsmen, breathing the ocean's pure air aboard the light cruisers.

The cruisers, to be sure, could exceed thirty knots and would leave the submarine far behind. But at 1:16 P.M. on September 12, the following radio message reached the *Casabianca:*

"The tenth division comprising *Fantasque* and *Terrible* has been delayed. Try to land at Ajaccio. A pilot will wait for you there beginning at 11:00 P.M., halfway between the Sanguinaires islands and Cape Muro. The pilot will display the reconnaissance letter 'P' as a signal, and you will reply with the letter 'F.' "

At 11:00 P.M. the *Casabianca* made contact with a pilot boat flying the colors of the Italian navy, much to l'Herminier's surprise. He has described what followed:

> That night, fires lit up the waves, and the setting was enchanting. The patriots undoubtedly had lit the fires for Saint-Jean's day, or had the Germans burned the *maquis?* The pale golden moon added a grandiose note to the scene.

We soon noticed the beacon, which was about 200 yards from the entrance, so we stopped.

A boat approached, and a Corsican pilot from Ajaccio came on board. He told me that we would have to put in at the Quai de la République, north of the harbor. I maneuvered so that the starboard would be on the quayside as we approached on the left.

Suddenly the sound of heavy firing broke the stillness. I began to reverse speed. But the pilot reassured me. "The square and the quay are full of people. All of Ajaccio is waiting for you. That noise was only the patriots celebrating. They're firing in the air to express their joy!"

L'Herminier found this most disconcerting.

"Is that how you waste the ammunition we have such a rough time transporting?" I asked.

"Tonight you'll have to forgive them, commander," the pilot answered.

"I gladly forgave them, but they sure gave us a scare!" said l'Herminier. His account continues:

The submarine pulled up at the quay. A clamor arose: "Long live France! Long live the *Casabianca!* Long live de Gaulle!"

At first our arrival caused some disappointment, for everyone was expecting the light cruisers that were to bring sizable reinforcements. The captain of the port had a large gangplank brought up, and we placed it in front of the cannon. Then, on our orders, the police pushed back the crowd, and a miracle of sorts occurred.

Three hatchways on the deck opened with a bang, and from them emerged three interminable lines of soldiers. They took possession of the square and managed to spread out so skillfully that they seemed ten times more numerous. I myself was fooled and began to wonder whether by some supernatural means we hadn't added a few men during the crossing.

The effect this produced on the population was dramatic. We were competing with the Trojan horse!

The arrival of the *Casabianca* in Ajaccio had scarcely been kept a dark secret, to put it mildly. Nor did the departure of the cruisers from Algiers occur a whit more discreetly, as Admiral Lepotier could testify: "The departure of the warships, overloaded with packing cases and soldiers in combat regalia, took place in the presence of an enthusiastic crowd. These onlookers responded with cheers to the chorus of shock troopers singing, 'You won't get Alsace and Lorraine,' as the ships reversed direction to leave the quay . . ."

During the night of September 13–14, the *Fantasque* and the *Terrible* completed their journey and landed 400 members of Commander Gambiez's shock battalion. Also on board were the new administrators appointed by the French Committee of National Liberation: Charles Luizet, recently named prefect of Corsica; General Mollard, the military governor; and Colonel Deleuze, General Martin's chief of staff.

On September 14 Colonel Deleuze left Ajaccio to go to Corte for a meeting with General Magli. After two hours of conversation, the atmosphere gradually grew more relaxed. Magli agreed that since the Germans were now the common enemy, the Italians ought to stop retreating and begin to fight back. With the help of the Corsican patriots, they must try to block a German advance across the mountains. Magli promised to hold the mountain area but prudently added that he could not answer for all his subordinates. He also agreed to tell the Italian commanders now in Ajaccio to pay a call on General Mollard. But he asked that the presence of French troops and Allied planes be demonstrated to the Italians.

Obviously, this was the real problem of the French command. And it was, for the moment at least, quite insoluble. The *Terrible*'s engines had suffered some damage on the return voyage to Algiers. The warships that had come from the Atlantic (the cruiser *Jeanne d'Arc,* the *Fortuné,* the *Basque*) did not return to Algiers until the 17th; the cruiser *Montcalm* was back in Oran on the 21st. The air force encountered even greater difficulties. Some Spitfires managed a quick trip to Camp del Oro but could not stay because there were no ground crews to provide supplies, maintenance, and defense.

For the time being, therefore, the scant resources of the insurgents and the small group newly arrived from Algeria had to suffice. While the strength of the shock battalion was being augmented by the addition of men from the Ajaccio region, the harassment of Nazi units was intensified throughout the interior of the island.

On the morning of September 10, the area military authorities summoned all the Maquis of the various cantons and distributed weapons and munitions. A series of attacks followed. A force of two hundred from Porta raided a munitions and oil depot in Champlan, and the enemy suffered heavy losses. On the same day, heavy firing shattered windows in Sartène. The Germans retreated to Bonifacio.

The fiercest skirmishes occurred in the village of Levie— population 3,000—thirteen miles northeast of Sartène. A convoy of eight German trucks passing through the village on September 10 was attacked and destroyed at ten in the morning. Six hours later twelve more trucks suffered the same fate. On September 12, two heavily armed convoys had to wage a considerable battle in order to traverse Levie. The Germans lost thirty men from each convoy.

During the night of September 14–15, after a forty-eight-hour respite, the Maquis learned that a formidable column was arriving from Bonifacio: fifty-five trucks transporting 1,200 men attached to a parachute division (German and Italian "Black Shirts"). The convoy was escorted by seven armored vehicles, including four twenty-three-ton "Sturmgeschütze" (75-millimeter guns mounted on automobile chassis).

The 200 Maquis of the village, who had perhaps a hundred

tommy guns, thirty grenades, and two German machine guns,
were commanded by Lieutenant Peretti of the 173rd Infantry.
The successes of the preceding days had made the blonde, blue-
eyed Corsican lieutenant the unchallenged leader of this small
group.

In Levie there was also a company of Italian infantry. Upon
learning of the Germans' impending arrival, the Italians decided
to retreat, but Peretti decided otherwise and forced them to stay.

Four cannon were placed in a firing position in the cemetery, a strategic point. The bridge at Roja, 700 yards from the
village, was mined and ready to be blown up. The Italians and
a group of Maquis hid nearby. The ravine spanned by the bridge
was covered by the two machine guns.

At six o'clock the German column reached the tunnel of
Bacino, ten miles south of Levie. The rough road rose over a
wild hillside between rocky cliffs. The Maquis of Sotta had tried
to blow up the tunnel with dynamite Peretti had given them.
The explosion caused some damage but failed to destroy the
tunnel, which was carved out of granite.

From their ambush, the patriots opened fire on the vehicles.
Three trucks were destroyed, but the rest of the convoy managed
to get through, crossed the Bacino pass, then the Ava pass, and
came down again around Carbini. Some twenty roadblocks consisting of large trees or rocks had been placed along the route.
As the Germans reached each roadblock, the Maquis opened
fire, but the heavily armed Germans forced them to yield.

The progress of the Germans as they drew closer to Levie
was carefully watched. When the convoy at last came within
range, the cannon opened fire, hitting several trucks. One,
loaded with ammunition, exploded.

At this point, the enemy called a halt for the night, but at
dawn the march resumed. Peretti had the bridge at Roja blown
up, and the Germans, using trench mortars, tried unsuccessfully
to cross the ravine. Hidden behind rocks on the opposite side,
the Maquis held firm.

The enemy rushed to the left of the defenders and soon reached the first houses of Levie. No trace could be found of the Italian troops. They had simply pulled back without further ado, and so Peretti ordered his own men to withdraw to the mountains.

André Maurois recalled the following episode in the fighting at Levie: "Jean Pandolfi was a boy of fifteen who had joined the patriots and obtained a tommy gun. All night long, exhibiting remarkable steadfastness, he had served as a liaison agent. Just as the attack on the convoy began, he was hit in the chest by a bullet. Peretti had him taken to the nearest hospital. Pandolfi bore up without complaint during the long ride over a rocky road. When he was finally put to bed, he said to his leader: 'My lieutenant, I am mortally wounded, I can sense it, but I've accomplished my mission and I'm happy to die for Corsica and for France!' He was given some brandy. 'I think I feel better,' he said. 'I guess I won't die after all. . . . My lieutenant, keep my tommy gun for me. I want to fight again . . .' Thereupon he breathed his last."

At Ajaccio, where enemy reconnaissance planes had been seen the day before, a certain anxiety prevailed. People had the feeling that the German advance in the south might pave the way for the arrival of larger forces. The batteries at Ajaccio were manned by Corsican sailors. All the cadres, including reservists and men demobilized after the dissolution of the Armistice Army, once again put on their uniforms and asked permission to serve.

The anxiety was of short duration. The enemy armored cars halted at the Roja bridge made no attempt to move on. The Germans evacuated Sartène as well as Levie and retreated to Porto-Vecchio.

It was also learned from the crew of an Italian ship arriving from Sardinia that this island had been almost completely evacuated by the German 90th Grenadier-Panzer Division. Clearly, the situation was improving.

In fact, as early as September 13 the German command had given up the idea of defending Corsica. General Senger und Etterlin received an order to transfer to the Continent all German forces (30,000 men, 10,000 from the Luftwaffe) still on the island. War matériel was to be moved through the port of Bastia. All personnel were to be flown out from the Ghisonaccia and Borgo-Bastia airports at the rate of 3,000 men a day. To meet the two-week deadline for the completion of operations, the Germans widened the Bastia bridgehead and assumed control of the mountain passes in the central part of the island. In addition, they had to cover the gradual evacuation of Bonifacio, Porto-Vecchio, and the entire coastal area in the east. This was the reason for the various German offensives.

During the night of September 16–17, the *Fantasque* and the torpedo-boats *Alcyon* and *Tempête* disembarked General Henry Martin and the Third Battalion of the Second Moroccan Riflemen, commanded by Boulanger. This unit relieved the original shock battalion, which now, despite its losses, was able to play a more important role.

During the night of September 20–21, the cruiser *Jeanne d'Arc,* the *Fantasque,* the *Alcyon,* and the *Tempête* disembarked General Louchet, commander of the Fourth Moroccan Alpine Division, a regiment of the First Moroccan Riflemen that included its first battalion, plus a battery of forty Bofors anti-aircraft guns, some radar equipment, and aviation gasoline. At the same time, an Italian cruiser brought thirty American commandos and an Englishman, General Peare, Eisenhower's personal representative, who was to transmit Allied orders to the Italians.

At dawn on September 21 a Glen Martin plane landed at Camp del Oro airport. To everyone's surprise, General Giraud emerged from it.

Giraud went immediately to General Magli's headquarters in Corte. He quickly spelled out the role the Italians were to play in the struggle against the Germans: to provide transport

—cars and muleteers—as well as other facilities the French lacked. Magli even agreed to put five artillery groups at the disposal of the Allies.

General Henry Martin has described the final plan of operations:

> Even though we could not completely contain the Germans, who were well equipped with armored vehicles, we could nonetheless do more with the kind of pressure tactics that apparently had proved so successful thus far. By threatening to deprive them of the port of Bastia, which they were using to evacuate most of their units and equipment, we would force them to act quickly and thus free Corsica all the sooner. They even might have to abandon some of their matériel and give up the idea of carrying out the extensive destruction they had planned. For this reason, we decided to attack Bastia as quickly as possible . . .

On October 4 the vanguard of the liberating troops entered Bastia. Because of a stupid lack of coordination at Allied headquarters, a tragedy marred the day. Unaware that the Germans had departed, American planes bombarded the city at ten in the morning, just as the people of Bastia were cheering their victorious soldiers. The American raid nearly destroyed Bastia's warehouses, something the Germans had planned to do but hadn't had time for. But Bastia had seen the last of the enemy, and Corsica was free.

CHAPTER SEVEN

~~~~~~~

THE MAKING
OF AN ARMY

O N OCTOBER 25, 1943, Marshal von Rundstedt, German
commander-in-chief in the west, presented a report that
summarized rather well the march of events in France:

> The changes in our military situation, exploited by enemy
> propaganda, have contributed to a growing feeling among the
> occupied peoples that we can no longer win the war. In the west,
> Resistance movements are on the increase. They are bigger,
> better organized, and better equipped. One of the principal
> reasons for this is the virulent opposition to forced labor in
> Germany. Resisters in large numbers are resorting to illegality.
> Many administrative and police officials in the occupied terri-
> tories are working against us by adhering to a policy of passive
> resistance. And the clandestine movements have been greatly
> helped by quantities of explosives and weapons parachuted from
> England. This explains the rapid increase in acts of sabotage
> against transport facilities and other targets: 534 such acts during

the month of September alone compared to a monthly average of 130 for the first half of 1943.

The aim of the Resistance movements and of the British organizations working with them is to set the stage for action against the rear of the German army to coincide with the Allied landings. Their most urgent task will be to attack our lines of communication with maximum force. Such is the danger inside the country, and it may have a very unfortunate effect in the course of a major battle. We can undoubtedly combat the Resistance movements effectively, but this will deplete our available forces and thus strengthen the position of the British and American troops.

Von Runstedt's uneasiness was based on very accurate information. He knew that the Maquis had grown substantially, especially in the mountainous regions. He also knew that its discipline had been considerably improved because many career officers had become available as a result of the disbandment of the Armistice Army, and they had rallied to the cause. The organization of sabotage operations was being perfected.

Sabotage in the S.N.C.F. (the French national railway company) had attained a unity of command through the creation of the *Bloc-Fer* (Rail Bloc), which later became a branch of the N.A.P. (*Noyautage des Administrations Publiques*).[1] It was René Hardy who achieved this unity of command and launched the sabotage program later known as the "green plan."

Bloc-Fer was directed nationally by Hardy, flanked by three aides: René La Combe, in charge of propaganda and screening personnel; Henri Garnier, military adjutant in charge of sabotage teams, who was in direct contact with the leaders of the Secret Army; and Max Heilbronn, technical adjutant. The latter had been a pioneer in that part of the Resistance movement which concentrated on railways. As early as 1941, he, together with

---

1. Editor's note: Meaning penetration of the public services, an organization whose purpose it was to infiltrate the civil service.

l'Estienne d'Orves, had worked out a plan for the sabotage of railroads. In every region, a *Chef-Fer* (Rail Chief) maintained close contact with the heads of the N.A.P. to whom he had to answer, with the services of the Secret Army whose military plans he had to implement, and with guerrilla groups who provided fighting personnel for immediate combat. Each region had its own intelligence as well as liasion communications services.

After René Hardy was arrested, Jean-Guy Bernard succeeded him as head of the *Bloc-Fer*. These resisters suffered heavy losses. The regional head for Lyon, J.-C. Thevenon, was arrested in October 1943. He died after being deported. The regional head for Limoges, A. Roiffet, was shot as a hostage in 1944. The regional head for Toulouse, Nentin, also was deported, and died. The same fate befell two others: L. Citroën, leader for the Marseille-Montpellier region, who was arrested in November 1943; and Jean-Guy Bernard, apprehended early in 1944.

In every instance, these leaders were replaced by others who likewise risked their lives until liberation. The railroad workers deserve all the more credit for what they did because they were often among the principal victims of Allied air raids.

The intensification of Allied bombing created a certain general uneasiness. Strategic requirements were not always understood by everyone, and of course even less by the families of the victims. During the year 1943, bombs leveled a number of cities in France. Many people were killed: 262 in Rennes on March 8; 200 in Rouen on March 12 and 28; 403 in Boulogne-Billancourt on April 14; 195 in Bordeaux on May 17; over 210 again in Rennes on the 29th; 280 in Le Creusot on June 20; 37 at Villacoublay and Le Bourget on July 14; 94 at Sochaux on the 15th; 110 at Le Bourget on August 16; 105 in Paris on September 3; 300 at Abbeville and St.-Omer on the 7th; 94 at Colombes and Nanterre on the 9th; 400 at Le Portel on the 10th; 301 at Courbevoie and Asnière on the 15th; 712 at Nantes on the 16th; 52 at Modane on the 18th; 500 again at Nantes on the

23rd; 450 at Toulon on November 24; 262 at Ivry, Bois-Colombes, Courbevoie and Asnière on December 31. In addition, over 7,500 people were wounded as a result of these bombardments.

There was no dearth of "well-meaning" people who openly declared that the bombs of their friends were as deadly and disagreeable as those of the enemy. They continued to talk this way even after the London radio sought to alleviate the psychological effect of these bombardments by announcing them in advance.

Certain Resistance leaders understood very well this aspect of the problem and even made use of it to justify their own actions. For example, in the clandestine newspaper *Libération Zone Sud* of October 30, the following exhortation appeared:

"Cut a railroad line, stop a locomotive, immobilize a factory, engage in sabotage always and everywhere. These represent additional steps toward victory; they obviate the need for more bombardments, and they will save many French lives."

The F.T.P. stepped up their local activities, with the drawback, already noted, of provoking the execution of numerous hostages. And yet all their operations still seemed to them to be insufficient. On August 6, 1943, the F.T.P. addressed the following message to de Gaulle:

> ... deficient in arms and explosives, we have to be stingy in using them and as a result must forgo a good many destructive actions that are definitely feasible. Sometimes we have no choice but to arm with a single pistol a whole group about to stage an attack. We are also compelled to hold the majority of our forces in reserve simply because we lack weapons.
>
> We're short of identity cards, food stamps, and money. We need them to guarantee the safety and material existence of our *Francs-Tireurs* and other resisters who rely on us.
>
> We lack the means of publicizing as widely as we should the heroic deeds of patriots fighting on French soil.
>
> We have often carefully detailed these needs to your delegates in France. They have made promises to us, and occasionally a start has been made toward carrying them out: three shipment

of arms and explosives, comprising one truckload in all; an amount of money that could keep one company alive for a month; radio broadcasts of some fragments of our communiqués. We do not hesitate to say that this is still far too little. If you agree to give us more weapons, we promise to use them well. As for the weapons themselves, it doesn't matter whether we receive them directly or through the intermediary of the Secret Army, provided they aren't allowed to remain in some depot where they might be seized by the police before we've had a chance to use them; provided we can use them right away in order to capture more arms from the enemy.

The Secret Army, meanwhile, was taking definitive shape despite the many intrigues that were being hatched both in Algeria and in metropolitan France.

In view of the large influx of young people in revolt against the S.T.O., the director of the M.U.R. had decided early in 1943 to set up a national service called simply "Maquis." On April 15 the directorate appointed Michel Brault, a Parisian lawyer, to head it. Brault set up headquarters in Lyon. On May 25 he drafted circulars establishing the Maquis's charter. Within one month, 20,000 copies of the text—which did not exceed the size of a playing card—were distributed throughout the southern zone.

The "Hercules" document of October 17, 1943, spelled out in detail the organization of the Secret Army:[2]

> The various Resistance movements, unified for military action, have contributed all their paramilitary formations to a single body—the Secret Army. This army comprises a number of services whose purpose is always the same: action against the enemy.
>
> A) The "immediate action" branch is ready to function right now by acts of sabotage and guerrilla warfare;
>
> B) That section of the Secret Army which is not slated for

---

2. Quoted by Guillain de Bénouville in *Le Sacrifice du Matin*.

immediate action will be asked to perform whatever duties the Inter-Allied Command demands of it on D-day.

The Secret Army is organized in accordance with a territorial division that has been determined by the Inter-Allied Command. It comprises, in addition to a national headquarters, twelve regions, most of which correspond to Vichy's regional divisions. Each region has its own headquarters that is made up of four offices. Each of these regional offices is under the direction of a Secret Army leader assisted by specialists concerned with immediate action, Maquis, troops reserved for D-day, etc.

The Secret Army's troops themselves are divided into:

1) Sixes—five men plus a leader of six.

2) Thirties—five groups of six plus a leader of thirty.

3) Hundreds—three groups of about thirty each plus a leader of 100 and a staff comprising one adjutant and at least four liaison agents, or 100 men in all.

The groups of 100 may be under the orders of a leader who is directly responsible to the departmental chief.

The departmental chief is under the orders of the regional general staff headed by a regional leader. The latter will have at his side a regional officer who, as a member of the French mission dispatched by the Inter-Allied Command, will be responsible for the implementation of any plan or action determined by that command.

Although he will not himself take over the command of the region he is assigned to, this officer will cooperate closely with the regional leader and the regional head of the Secret Army. All important decisions will be reached jointly. National headquarters will control and direct the activities of the regional general staff. The chief of the Inter-Allied Command mission will coordinate the activities of the regional and national echelons in accordance with directives from the Inter-Allied Command. Twelve regional officers together with the services responsible for parachute and landing operations will be under his orders.

The "Hercules" report paved the way for a meeting held in Geneva in October. Chaired by Guillain de Bénouville, the meeting was attended by Jussieu, chief of staff of the Secret Army; Louis Mangin, who served as national military delegate; Arrighi, representing the military heads of the northern zone's coordinating committee; Degliame, in charge of immediate action (*groupes francs* or irregular units and workers' action); and finally Magescas, delegate of the Maquis's national service.

On their way back, the delegates cautiously crossed the frontier by twos. The first to cross, Jussieu and Degliame, were arrested in Annemasse by the Gestapo. Because they carried large sums of money, the Germans took them for smugglers. Meanwhile, Guillain de Bénouville learned of their arrest and asked the N.A.P. to handle it. The customs service immediately asked that the smugglers be turned over to them. One of the N.A.P. resisters was dispatched to get them. Bénouville tells the story:[3]

> Taken to German headquarters and confronted with a Frenchman they took for a collaborator, Jussieu and Degliame bowed their heads. Our comrade of the N.A.P. didn't know how to make them realize who he really was.
>
> "So! There you are, Messieurs," he began severely. "Your story reminds me of *Pontcarrel*."[4]
>
> Degliame and Jussieu jumped at the mention of this word, because it was Jussieu's code name.
>
> "Well," the man concluded, very eager to alert them, "you've come to a sorry pass, as Barrès would say."
>
> When they heard my code name, the unfortunates no longer had any doubts. But then the N.A.P. man treated them so sternly that the next day, when the Germans delivered them to the French police, they were convinced they would be severely punished.

They were finally freed that same day, after paying a heavy fine. A few days later the Gestapo at Lyon got wind of the

---

3. *Le Sacrifice du Matin.*
4. A movie directed by Jean Dalannoy that was very popular at the time.

matter and learned through a telephone call to Annemasse that the two men had been freed. Because these members of the Annemasse Gestapo had allowed such big game to slip through their fingers, they were sent to the Eastern front. Needless to say, incidents of this kind rarely ended so well.

Sent to London via Spain on February 14, 1944, Michel Brault drafted a report listing the various elements available for action:

1) The "sedentaries" who comprised the Secret Army. "These are usually men who continue to lead a normal family and business life but who are organized into teams of 6, 30, and 100, and finally into battalions. Only a few of them are armed." In all, they totaled about 120,000 men (10,000 in each military region).

2) The *groupes francs*. "These units, formed on a regional basis, comprise either groups of six 'sedentary' specialists or carefully chosen members of the Maquis who have received special training. Included in the category listed in the preceding paragraph, the *groupes francs* consist of approximately 5,000 men, 2,000 of whom are 'sedentary' F.T.P.'s controlled by the Communists."

3) Maquis. "These include youths who have rebelled against the S.T.O. as well as men of all ages who have given up trying to live a normal life, either because they are being sought by the German or French police or because they voluntarily chose this kind of self-imposed exile within their own country." They totaled about 48,000.

Brault went on to provide additional details: "The maquisards are sometimes in camps only a few miles apart. Usually, however, they are widely dispersed over an entire department. There is not a single department in France that has more than 1,500 men living in camps, and not one containing fewer than 120 men (except for the Nord and Pas-de-Calais departments)."

In concluding, he stated quite positively: "The Secret Army of France is now in a position to contribute appreciable aid to

Allied aviation. This it will be able to do by organizing a program of immediate action and sabotage which, in my judgment, can be established and supervised only by a highly centralized body."

After Brault departed for Algiers, his adjutant, Georges Rabattet, succeeded him as the man charged with nationwide responsibility for the Maquis. André Favereau represented him in the northern zone.

The table of organization adopted by the Secret Army did not satisfy the Communists. The members of the F.T.P., who favored all-out guerrilla warfare, were especially critical. They felt that their projects were being blocked by the Allies. In this connection, their leader, Charles Tillon, has written:[5]

> The *attentiste* and reactionary leaders, whom de Gaulle and the American and British governments have appointed to control the Resistance for the benefit of their often contradictory interests, will try to extend their infiltration and their paralyzing pressure. They will demonstrate their hostility to the F.T.P., and this in turn will lead them to pursue a bankrupt strategy: that of pitting the larger Maquis against the guerrillas.

However, the disappearance of Jean Moulin, the arrest and deportation of Emile Bollaert, who had been appointed a delegate to the C.F.L.N. by de Gaulle in September 1943, and then the arrest and suicide of Pierre Brossolette—all of this redounded to the advantage of the Communists. To be sure, the C.N.R. had chosen Georges Bidault, a Christian Democrat, as its president. But since the C.N.R. was unable to hold plenary sessions, it had to delegate its powers to a committee of four, two of whom were Communists. Moreover, an Action Committee, the COMAC, was established to deal with military problems, and the Communists quickly dominated it. In addition, the Com-

---

5. *Les F.T.P.*, Juilliard, 1962.

munists had the sympathy of d'Astier de la Vigerie (though it must be said that they could not rely upon it), who was the C.F.L.N.'s commissioner for internal affairs after November 9, 1943.

For all these clandestine activists, the year 1943 was marked by a series of attacks against the enemy.

Thus, for example, reports received by the F.T.P. command listed the following for the period from April 1 to September 30: 270 operations against railways or railroad cars carrying German troops and matériel; the destruction of thirteen floodgates; eighteen attacks against enemy detachments; the disruption of two powerhouses, three substations and twenty-six transformers, etc. It was estimated that as a consequence of these actions, 950 Germans were killed and 1,890 wounded. And these were only partial figures because communication difficulties made it impossible to keep an exact tally.

The conflict over the correct approach to immediate action continued. Jacques Soustelle has commented on this:[6]

> Our Special Services favored immediate action, but on two conditions that made a good deal of sense: that the attacks be useful and consequently integrated into an overall plan: and that the means so employed should not be abstracted from the preparation of plans for destruction on D-day, especially the "green plan."

In London and Algiers the complaint against the Communists was precisely that they often acted alone. It was plain that unity of action was more necessary than ever before if the sabotage missions were to succeed and thereby help to limit the number of aerial bombardments.

With this in mind, de Gaulle's Special Services dispatched several sabotage teams to France. Objectives in every instance were determined by the Ministry of Economic Warfare. The

---

6. *Envers et Contre Tout*, Volume II.

French were eager to prove that the Allies themselves would benefit from such missions: their planes and pilots would be saved, and they would also avoid exasperating the civilian population.

Among these operations were the "Armada" missions (August-September and November-December 1943). Jarrot and Colonel Mary were their heroes, men who had helped several teams of Maquis and *groupes francs*.[7]

"Armada I" was designed to put out of commission the central power plants in Châlon-sur-Saône. Eighty percent of their electrical output went to Germany, twenty percent to the Creusot works.

At 6:00 P.M. on September 1, a team crossed the Saône River 1,700 yards from the power plants. The men hid in a thicket to ready their equipment. At 9:00 P.M. they began a slow and difficult approach to the target. One of the participants wrote:

> After reaching the big E station's large pylon on the Berne line, we placed our explosives twelve feet away. From there, protected by Pierre and two men with tommy guns, we then crawled toward the doors of stations C and D, which were about thirty-six yards from the main sentry post.
>
> I placed my explosives against the doors and close to the four beams that supported them. By 11:30 we had finished and went on toward the power plants. Twenty-two policemen and two Germans were doing sentry duty. The only possible point of entry for us was guarded by two policemen standing about eighty-five yards apart. In addition, we were severely hampered by a large floodlight that illuminated the spot. We crawled across the road on our bellies and managed to get over the first two barriers.

It took them another three-quarters of an hour to mine the transformers with explosives and delayed-action charges, and

---

7. Reports quoted by Jacques Soustelle.

then to retreat quietly and recross the Saône. But at a quarter to one, what fireworks! By then the sabotage team was two and a half miles away. Nevertheless, "it was as light as day outside."

Meanwhile, in Germolles and at the Creusot works, two other teams were mining the transformers and the "Henri-Paul Schneider" plant.

Here events occurred a little more rapidly than planned. The delayed time bombs were activated by heat from the transformers and went off too soon. The six saboteurs, who had no time to make a getaway, were suddenly surrounded by Germans. They owe their lives to the timely arrival of a car whose powerful headlights momentarily blinded the enemy. Taking advantage of the confusion, they managed to escape, leaving behind two bicycles and a few weapons.

The "Armada II" mission was aimed at the pylons of the main transmission lines from Eguzon to Paris, from Roye to Gennevilliers, and from Creney to Paris and to Kembs. The equipment had been dropped by parachute and was deposited in four depots, each receiving from two to four special metal containers that held approximately 440 pounds of plastic bombs, delayed bomb charges, and detonators.

During the night of November 8–9, Mary and Jarrot were parachuted to the Saône-et-Loire area with fourteen containers of equipment. The dry and precise account by Colonel Mary gives an idea of the extraordinary feats that were accomplished with so much aplomb:[8]

> On November 14, M. 24 (an imaginary designation), together with the local head of the Secret Army, visited the power station of the Blanzy mines. It was decided that the transformers would be blown up on the night of December 2–3. We still had to deliver the "merchandise" [the explosives], a task which an agent of the Intelligence Service managed to perform in spite of several barriers erected by the Germans.

---

8. In *Les Compagnons de la Grandeur.*

On the 15th and 17th, further deliveries of the "merchandise" in Châlon-sur-Saône, Chatenay, and Tournus. On the 18th, departure for Troyes and Paris . . .

On the 22nd, M. 24 went out to reconnoiter the Roye-Paris electric line. He decided to blow up seven large pylons at the exit of the very important station in Villiers-le-Bel, Gonesse. On the 23rd, thanks to a police permit, he was able to visit the Gennevilliers power station. He concluded that an attack was possible because the factory was guarded by only a few Germans and about fifteen policemen. On the 24th, passing through Epernay, he could see for himself the magnitude of the disaster that had occurred after the November 8–9 parachute drop: all the depots had been seized except for the one assigned to him, but he was unable to take possession of it because of the Gestapo's close surveillance.

On the 28th, M. 24 was at Soissons. Here he inspected the Saint-Quentin canal, then the Aisne canal, with an eye to blowing holes in the dam. He found two good landing fields for the parachute-dropping zone, Criptan and Poumon, and took notes to transmit to London.

On the 29th and 30th, "merchandise" transported from Reims to Troyes by train and truck. There was a certain degree of risk, but the result was a complete success.

On December 1, M. 24 arrived in Troyes. Thanks to his police pass, he entered the Créney power station, which was guarded by 250 Germans. He ascertained where the D.C.A. batteries were located and where the sentries were posted, then assessed the risks of an attack.

On December 2 he learned that a factory in Troyes repaired submarine Diesel engines. He immediately went to the factory, inspected the engines, prepared thirty-six sticks of dynamite for the thirty-six repaired engines, and asked the head of the Saône-et-Loire branch of the Secret Army to carry out the expedition at once. That very evening this man managed to get into the factory, but he was nervous, handled himself badly, and the expedition was a failure.

At 6:00 P.M. the same day, M. 24 took two men and left

for the hamlet of Marney, two miles from Créney, where he planned to blow up some pylons he had inspected twenty-four hours earlier. It was pouring rain all day. M. 24 personally set the charges on pylon 22, an enormous structure holding all the lines as well as nine secondary pylons.

On the morning of December 3, the pylons blew up. M. 24, having instructed the Troyes team to repeat the performance as soon as the repairs had been completed, left for Châlon-sur Saône.

At Montceau-les-Mines, the attempt to blow up the power station failed owing to the arrest of comrades who had talked after being subjected to torture. In agreement with the local leader, M. 24 planned another attempt for December 5, one that would take longer but hopefully would succeed.

Passing through Ciry (where he blew up three locomotives in the station) and then Mary, where he damaged two large pylons, M. 24 reached Lyon.

These few facts show how complex were the missions assigned to agents of the B.C.R.A. and also how liaison was established with the Maquis.

In the continuing development of the Maquis, the most significant and also the most moving incidents occurred in the town of Oyonnax, in the Ain *département,* toward the end of 1943.

The Maquis had begun to organize in the Ain in December 1942. At that time there were only small groups of young rebels against the S.T.O. Taking refuge on farms, they relied on false identity cards. They had neither weapons nor money. A committee was formed at Saint-Rambert to collect gifts in cash and in kind that would enable these clandestine youths to subsist.

Little by little, the local Maquis expanded its organization. A training school was opened at Gorges above Mongriffon in June 1943. Captain Romans, leader for the Ain, has described the situation:

The watchwords were explicit: no large concentrations of men. No pitched battles. Guerrilla warfare only! We had only a few revolvers and some hunting rifles and were reduced to making sketches in order to teach the use of modern weapons. Early in July we finally received our first Sten machine gun. We kept taking it apart and putting it together until we could do it in record time. Then the gun was passed from one camp to another. On July 14 two delegates from the regional headquarters came to Gorges to inspect. From then on, the Ain Maquis became part of the Secret Army, and its survival was to some extent guaranteed.

By October 1 ten camps were in operation. Several raids enabled them to obtain some needed supplies. An old Citroën truck christened "Maquisette" provided the ideal means of transport whenever quick action was called for.

On September 29 the Maquis carried out a most daring nocturnal expedition against the warehouses of the local authorities in Bourg, despite the fact that the city was infested with Germans and militiamen. Forty-five tons of precious supplies were seized without a shot having been fired. It took at least nine trucks to cart the loot away. The Germans failed to react because they thought that such a convoy of armed men must be an official one.

On November 11, Captain Romans pulled off a master stroke: he took over the town of Oyonnax for the purpose of celebrating the 1918 armistice in fitting fashion. Guillain de Bénouville explained that Romans "had decided to organize this public demonstration because Philippe Henriot's[9] radio campaign was affecting adversely the Maquis's relations with the civilian population, who were frightened by all the tales of crime and terror. Henriot, in alluding to Romans, told his listeners that the leader of the band in the Ain was a Russian Jew who had escaped from the ghetto."

Romans chose the town of Oyonnax for certain special reasons. Most of its 15,000 inhabitants were sympathetic to the Maquis. Not many German troops were stationed there. It was

9. A right-wing politician and leading Nazi collaborator.

close to Nantua, where Verchier, the local police chief, belonged to the Resistance and could therefore provide assistance.

To make sure that everyone's attention would be focused on Nantua, some resisters even put up posters announcing that a demonstration would take place in the town on November 11. With understandable eagerness, Verchier called this to the attention of the prefecture and asked for all available reinforcements. And so the Vichy forces were stationed ten miles from the actual scene!

The enemy control commissions stationed at Oyonnax were being transferred, which resolved that problem. In addition, Romans had a trump card up his sleeve: Thévenon, the town's police commissioner, with whom he had reviewed every eventuality well beforehand. The two men even reconnoitered on foot the route the parade would follow.

In the camps, the men knew only one thing: they were going to march in a parade on November 11. But they did not know where.

Transported to town in two trucks, the first Maquis groups took over Oyonnax without striking a blow. Lieutenant Bourret, commander of the security teams, entered the post office: "We're the Maquis! Hands up!"

The policeman on duty hid under a table. The telephone exchange was now in the hands of the Maquis, and thanks to the complicity of Curtis, the head of the post office, it remained under their control. The same was true of other public buildings. The Maquis maintained order. All the municipal policemen were disarmed, including, naturally, the police commissioner. And a lookout was maintained for anyone or anything that appeared suspect.

Following the prearranged itinerary, fourteen trucks arrived, depositing approximately 300 men in front of the post office. The people were stunned. The Maquis were invading the streets of the town in the full light of morning!

Romans got out of his car and snapped: "The Ain Maquis, under my command. Attention!"

The crowd went wild with enthusiasm. "Long live the Maquis! Long live de Gaulle!" they shouted. The parade got under way, preceded by bugles and drums. Romans was flanked by the regional and departmental chiefs of the Secret Army. A guard of honor, wearing white gloves, gathered around the flag.

On the black-draped monument to the dead, Romans placed the Cross of Lorraine. It bore the following inscription: "From the victors of tomorrow to those of yesterday."

After taps were played for the dead, everyone lustily sang the *Marseillaise,* then the *Lorraine March.*

Guillain de Bénouville has described the scene:

> The people, in tears, crowded around the resisters, hugged them, gave them money—5-, 10-, 1,000-franc notes, and all the cigarettes they happened to have on them. An elderly man asked Romans's permission to embrace him, saying, "You have avenged the death of my son, who was killed in '40."
>
> A little old lady knelt at his feet and kissed his hand. I shall never in all my life forget this day—the joy, the emotion of the population. All those Frenchmen gathered together in one place were so proud of one another.

But of course the demonstration could not last too long. Romans asked everyone to do nothing that might provoke the Germans to take retaliatory action. He went back to his car and, now that he was alone, began to weep. Bénouville adds:

> He couldn't contain his tears. For nights he had been unable to sleep because he was worried about the Germans' reaction and the possibility that hostages would be seized in retaliation. But now he had achieved his goal. He had demonstrated to men, women, and children that his men were true Frenchmen, good Frenchmen, and that they had the air of fine people, not of bandits.

The Germans would stoop to anything to discredit the "terrorists." One of the most active groups of the F.T.P. in the Paris region was commanded by an Armenian, Manouchian, and comprised three Frenchmen, eight Polish immigrants, five Italians, three Hungarians, two Armenians (including Manouchian), one Spaniard, and one Russian. When this group was rounded up, Nazi propaganda tried to exploit the xenophobia of the people. Posters were put up on every wall proclaiming: "Liberators? Liberation by an army of criminals!"

The twenty-three men were sentenced to death on February 21, 1941. Then the posters were covered with inscriptions glorifying the "terrorists" and with strips of paper bearing the words, "They died for France."

The time had now come to give status to the armed forces of the Resistance. In March 1944 General de Gaulle established the "French Forces of the Interior" (F.F.I.), which included all clandestine troops. He directed that they be organized so far as possible into regular military units: platoons, companies, battalions, regiments. And he decreed that each of their commanding officers be given an appropriate temporary rank.

In his *War Memoirs,* the General noted: "One could certainly predict that, with wild extravagance, all sorts of stripes would be sewn on berets and sleeves which reclassifying commissions would later have to sort out. But by organizing the groups in the traditional manner—which they themselves very much desired—I made sure that in the end French unity would be served."

In April, General Koenig, the hero of the battle of Norway and of Bir Hakeim, was appointed commander of the F.F.I. De Gaulle sent him to England to serve with Eisenhower. "It was from there," wrote the head of the Free French, "that he could best activate the Resistance, coordinating its movements with our joint strategy, communicating with it through all available channels, and providing it with needed arms and other support."

These were decisive steps toward the creation of the new national army.

~~~~~~~~

CHAPTER EIGHT

THE GLIÈRES
BATTALION:
A SYMBOL

AN EPISODE OF the greatest symbolic importance for the Resistance, involving as it did direct military confrontation with the enemy, occurred early in 1944 in Haute-Savoie.

The Maquis of Haute-Savoie had become increasingly well organized, trained, and equipped as 1943 progressed. With the arrival of winter and heavy snow, the leaders of the Secret Army faced a problem: should they force the Maquis to remain idle in its hideouts, or should they run the risk of exposing it to the danger of speedy capture by the authorities, who would have an easy time following fresh tracks made in the snow?

The decision was made in London. Members of the Maquis were to be grouped in a zone that the enemy would have a hard time reaching but where they could be provisioned. It must be an area accessible for parachute drops. The Glières plateau was the perfect answer. No road led to the Glières plateau. The few footpaths that existed were narrow and winding. It was a veritable mountain bastion, six miles wide, surrounded by the Thônes, Thorens, and Borne valleys.

In January 1944 the Secret Army ordered the Maquis to assemble on the Glières plateau. The F.T.P. were asked to join them.

On the evening of January 29, the first 120 members of the Haute-Savoie Maquis began the climb to the plateau. They were led by a twenty-eight-year-old lieutenant, "Tom" (Théodose) Morel, an officer of the Alpine *Chasseurs*.

What did these men who deliberately left for the glacial solitude of the Savoy hideout look like? Lieutenant Jourdan describes them:

"The men of the Maquis were certainly a picturesque lot. The group from the Manigod region, all of them soldiers who had joined the fight early, enjoyed the privilege of wearing the uniform of the *Chasseurs,* complete with fur-lined vests. You could scarcely tell them apart from regular troops. The men from the Bouchet area wore tunics and pants taken when we raided the Vichy depots; two or three were in sailor's uniform, others wore sweaters and bits of khaki. The majority, however, wore civilian clothes, with the Savoy beret over one ear."

The headquarters of the command post were set up in a sizable cottage that also housed members of the guard, liaison agents, and, eventually, guests. Elsewhere on the post, a number of huts were earmarked for various officers, the infirmary, and custodians of munitions. All in all, about forty huts, which ordinarily sheltered the herds during the summer months, were used.

Four companies, comprising from forty to seventy men divided into several platoons, were placed under the command of Lieutenants Jourdan-Joubert, Forestier, Humbert, and Lamotte. Each platoon was assigned the duty of watching over a specific area and defending it if need be. It was plain that there were not enough men to encircle the plateau completely. In fact, the platoons were quite far apart from one another. To compensate for this, Tom Morel set up a ski scout service. Twenty-five hand-picked youths were given powerful weapons— but they had no skis! That was no problem: a quick raid on neighboring ski resorts garnered some first-rate equipment at the expense of tourists for whom the war was not an overriding concern.

Soon, at the direction of Captain Humbert Clair, departmental head of the Secret Army, various regional groups began the climb to Glières. The F.T.P. of Grand-Bornand, whose equipment even included a field telephone, arrived. Another group of forty-three F.T.P.s swelled the numbers. Fifty-six Spaniards, veterans of the republican army who had escaped just as they were about to be handed over to the Germans for deportation, decided to join the Maquis. They were grouped into a separate contingent called the "Ebro" platoon. Members of the *corps francs* from Thônes, no longer able to remain in the valley because they were too well known to the police, also took the road to Glières. By February 20 the Glières forces had increased from 120 to 465.

From the outset, the most pressing problem was that of feeding all these men, isolated on a plateau with no supplies save unseasoned wood, frozen potatoes, and a few cows. Their very survival was at stake. During the first days, columns of ten to fifteen sleds could be seen carrying food supplies from Essert to the plateau. But this soon had to be discontinued. After the police arrived in the Borne valley, groups of men were organized to bring food up on their backs. But despite the strenuous efforts of all concerned—the peasants, in particular, were helpful—the situation soon became quite critical.

Furthermore, there remained the twin problems of liaison and security. The Maquis, of course, had innumerable contacts with people who helped to gather information. But even though the Germans as yet had little knowledge of what was transpiring at Glières, the threat of enemy infiltration was a constant concern. The Maquis of Glapigny, near Thônes, had recently had a very painful experience. Lieutenant Jourdan-Joubert has told the story:[1]

> A young Belgian had joined the Maquis, and it didn't take him long to make friends. He claimed that the Gestapo had murdered all the members of his family. But one day an S.S. identity card was found on his person. His shoes were promptly removed, and he was held prisoner in the hope that he would end up by talking. But no one could get a word out of him. So it was decided to execute him.
>
> One after the other, his comrades backed away from the job. Still, they needed one man to volunteer to kill the spy, so one was appointed: "You, so-and-so, you've already killed a Boche. It's up to you to do it." So-and-so had to agree. He seized his tommy gun and looked at his former comrade: "Will you forgive me?" "Of course," was the reply. The two men embraced. "But then," so-and-so related, "I couldn't kill him." They all stood there, completely at a loss. "Well, it's not up to me to give you courage," the doomed man said. "Hurry up!" At this point, the lieutenant intervened. He fired, but the bullet missed the man's chest and entered his shoulder. The wounded man removed from his pocket a blood-stained pouch and asked that it be sent to his mother. A bullet to the heart finally finished him off. With the disappearance of the spy went his secret. All he would say was, "I'm sorry I couldn't pull it off."

And so a continuous watch was maintained at Glières. No allusions to any activity were permitted in the men's correspondence, which was taken to the Annecy post office regularly. Anyone who came up to Glières was not allowed to go back down. Contact with the outside world was maintained solely through liaison agents.

---

1. A member of the 27th B.C.A., Jourdan-Joubert, together with Julien Helfgott and Pierre Golliet, wrote *Glières,* a book published by the association of Glières survivors.

In mid-February the first parachute drop was made to the plateau. The Maquis received both guns and automatic pistols. Lieutenant Jourdan-Joubert noted proudly: "Our Allies are treating us like soldiers."

During the night of March 4–5, two planes dropped thirty containers. On March 10 thirty planes dropped 580 containers, or about ninety tons of matériel. The operation lasted four hours, and it took several days to recover all the containers.

In February an incident had occurred which had the most critical consequences. Five members of the Maquis who had just obtained some food supplies at a farm were driving away in a car which broke down near the bridge over the Borne at Essert. Unable to start the car, they decided to push it across the bridge to the other side. They were in the middle of the bridge when a detachment of the Vichy police *Gardes mobiles* appeared. Taken by surprise, the men lost their heads and ran, firing their guns as they went. The head of the *Gardes* detachment immediately issued an order to return the fire. One maquisard was wounded but managed to escape with a comrade. The other three were taken prisoner.

News of this encounter quickly reached Abbé Truffy, the curate of Petit-Bornand and a courageous resister. Two of the captives were members of his parish, which gave him an excuse to intervene. After going through various chains of command, the abbé finally went to the Villa Mary in Annecy, where Colonel Georges Lelong had his headquarters. The departmental head of the Vichy police force did not mince words:[2]

"You have some very turbulent parishioners, it seems."

"A few hotheads, my colonel, but good Frenchmen all the same."

"Unfortunately, we are living in an era when opinions vary about the meaning of such words as 'good Frenchmen.' But one

---

2. *Le Bataillon des Glières*, by Michel J. Bird, Editions France-Empire.

thing is certain: In firing on the *Gardes* from the bridge, your fine fellows and the others too have started something that none of us may be able to stop."

Abbé Truffy feigned surprise. "I really don't understand, my colonel. Why should this be so?"

"Because my men were pursuing Lamouille and his gang— no one else. Now, of course, that is no longer the situation, because in chasing down a dozen criminals we have uncovered something far more serious. Moreover, when the Germans received our report about the bridge incident, they too began to realize the gravity of the situation."

More important, on January 10 Lamouille and his gang had entered Bonneville and seized the inspector and ten other policemen who had orders to arrest them.

The gang leader's plan was to negotiate directly with Vichy for the liberation of a few Communist members of the Maquis who had previously been captured by the militia. To prove that the policemen he held were still alive, he freed one hostage and sent him to Vichy. Laval himself interrogated the man. The policeman declared that the F.T.P. would not hesitate to kill all his comrades, but Laval refused to consider the proposal of an exchange of prisoners. Instead, he ordered the start of operations against the "terrorists" of Haute-Savoie.

Anticipating Laval's reaction, Captain Clair made a last-ditch attempt to persuade the F.T.P. in Lyon to order the release of his captives. The F.T.P. leaders refused, saying it was not their habit to oppose any decision reached by their local delegates.

On January 20 the F.T.P. group left the chalet where they had taken cover. A few weeks later, the corpses of the luckless policemen were discovered in a ditch near Saint-Laurent.

Lelong, who was fiercely hostile to the F.T.P. and all it stood for, did not seem to harbor harsh feelings toward the Secret Army. His conversation with the abbé appeared to indicate this.

On February 10, the day that the abbé came to ask for the

release of the three imprisoned maquisards, Lelong still had no very clear idea of the real strength of the forces on the Glières plateau. More important, he did not know that these included an F.T.P. contingent. Assuming that Abbé Truffy enjoyed the trust of the Resistance, Lelong asked him to relay a message to the Glières leaders: "Tell them to leave the plateau immediately and go home. I shan't ask them to hand over their weapons, and I give you my word that they will not be molested. But they'll have to come down from Glières in order to avoid running into my people. I'll then be able to send a negative report to the Germans telling them they've been misinformed. This will satisfy them. Once they've been reassured, the Secret Army will be able to regroup. I promise not to interfere provided they do nothing to draw attention to themselves."

As a token of his good faith, he agreed to free the three young men captured at Essert.

The next day, February 11, Colonel Lelong was summoned to the Villa Schmidt, headquarters of the German police, to attend a meeting presided over by Hauptsturmführer Jeewe. That same evening, Jeewe sent the following telegram to the S.S. regional commander in Lyon:

> According to information obtained in the course of preliminary operations, it is obvious that some Secret Army groups have retired to the Glières plateau southeast of Thorens, southwest of Petit-Bornand, and north of Thônes. Colonel Lelong has decided to encircle and attack the plateau. Preparations were started today at 6:00 P.M. Three groups, A, B, and C, are participating. They comprise nine squadrons of the *Garde mobile,* three squadrons of *Garde mobile* reservists, and 200 members of the militia. Group A, under the orders of squadron leaders Colomb and Raulet, will march on Petit-Bornand and Bonneville, in the south; Group B, commanded by Brenod of the G.M.R. [*Garde Mobile* reservists], will leave from Thorens and bear east; Group C, under Captain Ney of the Militia, will head north from Faverges for the Glières plateau.

This is not, for the moment, an offensive action. Its purpose is reconnaissance and encirclement. The three groups have been ordered to seal off the region and keep it under strict surveillance. Moreover, we will set up bases to give us access to the plateau prior to launching the general attack at a date to be determined.

During the night, a liaison agent came to Glières to bring news of the G.M.R.'s forthcoming incursion. Tom Morel sent orders to the "Savoie-Lorraine" platoon: "A detachment of G.M.R. are coming up to Essert this morning to reconnoiter the plateau. Ambush them."

The *Garde mobile,* taken by surprise, were reduced to firing blindly, whereas their adversaries were firmly entrenched on terrain that was perfectly familiar to them. Only mercy saved the *Gardes* from being killed to the last man.

But the *Garde mobile* suffered heavy casualties: one officer and three men killed, three wounded. All the others were forced to surrender to the Maquis to avoid being slaughtered. They were released after being relieved of their weapons, except for three men held as hostage for the three men captured at Essert. Tom did not know at that point that Abbé Truffy had already arranged for the maquisards' release.

Colonel Lelong learned of this turn of events while he and Jeewe were making a tour of inspection. He arrived at Petit-Bornand in high dudgeon only to find the abbé busy tending the wounded.

The two men talked things over. Finally, Lelong said: "Several of my officers, especially those in the militia, have already protested the release of the prisoners in return for your assurances that they would behave themselves. My officers say they cannot trust you because you are collaborating with the Resistance. I'm afraid that today's happening will only serve to increase their suspicions. Therefore, in order to protect both sides, I'm going to take steps to curtail your activities. I will ask you, however, to continue your efforts to obtain the release of my three men who were captured today."

In any event, Hauptsturmführer Jeewe was not fooled. After a report of the day's events, he cabled that same evening:

> The militia's reconnaissance of the last few days has definitely uncovered the presence on the plateau of Glières of a large group of Maquis from the Haute-Savoie. Moreover, it is plain that they are prepared to defend their installation vigorously. On Wednesday 2/9/44, as a patrol approached, many men were seen moving into previously prepared positions.
>
> According to what I was told yesterday by Captain Vaugelas and Lieutenant Constanzo of the militia, the plateau is virtually unapproachable because of the snow. In addition, experience has taught us that we can only attack by using heavy artillery, should it be possible to bring it up here and position it advantageously in this snowy weather. It would be preferable—and this is the hope of the militia—to attack by air.

On February 13 Captain Anjot of the Secret Army paid a visit to Abbé Truffy. Anjot listened to the abbé's report of his meeting with Colonel Lelong and promised that Lelong's suggestion would be carefully considered. On February 15 Tom Morel let it be known that he was prepared to release the three members of the *Garde mobile* if someone would take charge of them on the plateau and guide them on their way down. Truffy himself volunteered for this mission. By 6:30 P.M. the three men were back in Petit-Bornand.

Meanwhile, Anjot, intrigued by Lelong's suggestion, had taken it upon himself to call on the colonel at his headquarters in Annecy. In a letter to Captain Clair he told of the steps he had taken.

> No need to give you all the details, but last night I saw Colonel Lelong, the police superintendent. It's absolutely necessary for you to come tomorrow morning if we are to reach some kind of understanding with the M.O. [*Maintien de l'Ordre*]. I believe that something can be accomplished. Come back with the two trusted agents who have brought you this note. You must be at

Essert no later than nine o'clock. On your way down, you'll find me somewhere between Ville and Entremont. The munitions and equipment must be returned to the *Gardes* immediately. In my opinion, this is a gesture we should make; it will compensate to a small degree for yesterday's incident. If necessary, bring these munitions down with you and the matter will thus be settled quickly. My interview with Lelong must remain a strict secret between you and Tom.

Tom Morel, for his part, had met with the commander of the *Gardes mobiles* group "Aquitaine" at La Clusaz. He had protested the barricades erected along the road used by the Maquis to bring up food. The officer reassured him, "My young friend, you talk a good deal but you don't use your eyes. We were ordered to barricade the paths leading to the plateau and we've done so. But all the same, I don't believe this will in any way hinder you, for we've issued no orders regarding the unobstructed terrain on either side of the barricades. Take a look for yourself and tell your people that they can come down peacefully through the snow. They'll be challenged only on the paths."

This was true of the *Gardes* but not of the G.M.R. or the militia. Besides, even if it was just a gesture, Lelong had had notices posted everywhere on January 31 which hardly inspired confidence among the Maquis. They read:

I hereby remind you that anyone caught with a weapon in his hand or anyone in possession of weapons or explosives will be brought before a court-martial immediately; he will be sentenced without any right of appeal and executed within forty-eight hours.

Negotiations were continued nevertheless until the very end. On February 21, at 10:00 P.M., Captain Clair met Colonel Lelong in a vacant house at La Louvatière. The man in charge of "the maintenance of order" repeated the proposals he had made to Anjot. These tallied with the instructions received from the Vichy government: the Secret Army was to negotiate with him independently and, in return for his guarantee, was to withdraw from the plateau without informing the Communists of its plans.

Clair considered these proposals unacceptable. He believed that the Gaullists needed the help of the Communist Party far more than it needed theirs. Besides, not one of the Glières fighters would consent to such an act of betrayal.

Lelong went so far as to promise the Secret Army that he would accept any conditions it laid down for withdrawal, provided that the F.T.P. were excluded. But Clair remained adamant. By one o'clock in the morning it was evident that the negotiations had failed.

On February 28 Tom Morel succeeded in contacting Commander Lefèvre, the new Vichy chief of the Entremont sector. He appealed to Lefèvre's patriotism, but to no avail. Lefèvre was the kind of officer who never questioned orders. Finally Tom did obtain one concession: the commander promised not to arrest anyone sent down to the valley for medication. Because the promise was given reluctantly, Tom did not believe he could rely on it.

The medical services, admittedly modest, were directed by Dr. Marc Bombiger, formerly attached to the Alpine *Chasseurs*. His assistant, Michel Fournier (called Michou), was a twenty-one-year-old who had studied medicine in Paris before joining the Secret Army. Lacking equipment, the two men had to improvise as best they could. Nonetheless, they managed admirably. A week after they had moved onto the plateau, all the hut leaders were invited to a housewarming. There they were proudly shown the infirmary with its red cross, entrance hall, refectory kitchen, operating room, surgery ward, and above all a huge stable transformed into a dormitory with its parachute container converted into a wooden stove and its "bathtub" a huge metal feeding trough propped up over a woodfire—a real luxury at Glières.

On March 1 Michel Fournier was arrested by the G.M.R. while on his way down to Grand Bornand to fetch bandages. Everyone at Glières was deeply devoted to Michou, whose gentleness, dedication, and perpetual good humor were well known.

When Tom learned that the promise made to him had been broken, he summoned all the company commanders and announced that he intended to attack Saint-Jean-de-Sixt, where Fournier was being held. The execution of his plan was entrusted to Lieutenant Humbert, whose company was lodged closest to the village.

At midnight the "Allobroges" and "Liberté chérie" platoons began their descent to the valley. Three hours later they reached Saint-Jean. The attack took the G.M.R. by surprise—so much so that the sentries had no time to sound the alarm. Within the space of half an hour the village was completely occupied without a shot having been fired. Reduced to helplessness, the G.M.R. were locked up in a school building. But Fournier was not in Saint-Jean. The police had transferred him to Annecy. Thereupon, Humbert telephoned Colonel Lelong.

"We'll free your G.M.R.s in exchange for the release of Fournier."

"All right. I'll issue the necessary orders."

"On your word of honor as an officer?"

"Yes."

But Lelong could not keep his promise. Fournier had already been handed over to the Germans by their overzealous collaborators. The Maquis, unable to forgive this act of treachery, decided to avenge Fournier.

On March 8 a plane appeared in the sky over Glières, sent by the Luftwaffe to take reconnaissance photos. An attack was apparently in the offing. Moreover, Glières was so completely encircled that food was becoming scarce. The men on the plateau had only a one-day supply of rice, beans, and frozen potatoes.

The arrival of Lamouille and his men on March 7 had increased the number of mouths to feed but in no way improved morale. On the contrary, opinions were divided; some regarded the newcomers as little better than a gang of criminals. As always, however, Tom Morel showed himself to be generous, saying: "Every man, as long as he is willing to give his life for France, is welcome here regardless of what he has done in the past. These men say they are prepared to make the supreme sacrifice if called upon to do so. They also agree to submit to our discipline. That's all I ask."

At 5:00 P.M. on March 9 Tom Morel met the platoon leaders to finalize plans for an attack on the G.M.R. of Entremont and to map out the details of its execution.

Lieutenant Jourdan-Jourbert has written:

> The attack was something new in the lives of the Maquis, who until now had been reduced to defensive action. This was to be no small-scale assault; rather, it involved most of our men, all of them eager to fight.

The surprise attack, scheduled to start at 2:00 A.M., was to be directed against all the G.M.R. posts.

"I don't want any bloodshed," Tom Morel declared.

At 11:30 the 100 men selected for the raid set out, with Tom himself in the lead. One of the participants, Clément Gérard, has recounted:

> After a long noiseless march, we reached the outskirts of Entremont. The light of the rising moon glistened on the snow and was reflected on us. We really could have done without that! We reached the G.M.R.'s posts, quickly crossed the barricades, and entered the grounds. Our orders were conveyed by signs rather than by words. A strong wind, however, suddenly arose and banged the loosely fastened shutters. A dog barked. I heard a comrade mutter: "You bastard, you'll give us away."
>
> A floodlight suddenly came on. Not far away, a voice could be heard. Police whistles sounded the alarm. One member of our

group was discovered. The pale rays of the floodlight shone over the sentry posts, went out and came on again, as piercing as a knife. We had to cross to the other side of the road. One by one we jumped over. All of a sudden we were trapped in the lights and plainly visible. Fifty yards away a voice boomed: "Halt! We're the police!" At the same time a volley of shots resounded. No one moved. We buried our heads in the snow.

The men sought protection behind a house, then resumed their advance. In the distance the sound of automatic rifles could be heard.

Triggered by the dog's barking, the fighting had begun fifteen minutes ahead of schedule. Tom Morel's platoons, which were to have seized the Hôtel de France, headquarters of most of the G.M.R.'s forces, had not yet reached their assault positions. As they entered the village, they were caught off guard by a powerful machine-gun barrage.

To prevent vacillation on the part of younger maquisards who had never before fought a real battle, Tom immediately urged them on to attack the hotel. Their daring paid off. No bullets struck them, and soon they were in control of the Hôtel de France.

Lefèvre, the Vichy commander, was there in the midst of his men. He asked permission to retain his revolver, in order to preserve his honor as an officer. He was allowed to keep it.

Tom Morel now urged him to order the surrender of the entire garrison, saying, "Your men will be freed after giving up their weapons and handing over their food and provisions." He added: "But you and your officers will have to go back up to Glières with us. We will keep you as hostages in order to obtain the release of Michel Fournier."

"If I order my men to lay down their arms, who will guarantee that you and your terrorists won't massacre all of us and throw our bodies into a ditch?" Lefèvre asked.

"You have my word," Tom replied. "And you also have my

The mathematics of totalitarianism: After the military governor of Nantes was killed, fifty Frenchmen were killed. This notice advises that fifty more will be killed if those responsible are not caught within forty-eight hours. It also offers a sizable reward for cooperation.

BEKANNTMACHUNG

Nach eingehender Beobachtung des Verhaltens der französischen Bevölkerung im besetzten Gebiet habe ich festgestellt, dass der Grossteil der Bevölkerung in Ruhe seiner Arbeit nachgeht. Man lehnt die von englischer und sowjetischer Seite gegen die deutsche Besatzungstruppe angezettelten Attentate, Sabotageakte usw. ab, weil man genau weiss, dass sich die Folgen dieser Ha..dlungen ausschliesslich auf das friedliche Leben der französischen Zivilbevölkerung auswirken.

Ich bin gewillt der französischen Bevölkerung mitten im Kriege weiter unbedingt Ruhe und Sicherheit bei ihrer Arbeit zu gewährleisten. Da ich aber festgestellt habe, dass den Attentätern Saboteuren und Unruhestiftern gerade von ihren engeren Familienangehörigen vor oder nach der Tat Hilfe geleistet wurde, habe ich mich entschlossen, nicht nur die Attentäter, Saboteure und Unruhestifter selbst bei Festnahme, sondern auch die Familien der namentlich bekannten aber flüchtigen Täter, falls diese sich nicht innerhalb von 10 Tagen nach der Tat bei einer deutschen oder französischen Polizeidienststelle melden, mit den schwersten Strafen zu treffen.

Ich verkünde folgende Strafen:

1.) Erschiessung aller männlichen Familienangehörigen auf- und absteigender Linie sowie der Schwager und Vettern vom 18. Lebensjahr an aufwärts.

2.) Überführung aller Frauen gleichen Verwandtschaftsgrades in Zwangsarbeit.

3.) Überführung aller Kinder der von vorstehenden Massnahmen betroffenen männlichen und weiblichen Personen bis zum 17. Lebensjahr einschliesslich in eine Erziehungsanstalt.

Ich rufe daher jeden auf, nach seinen Möglichkeiten Attentate, Sabotage und Unruhe zu verhindern und auch den kleinsten Hinweis, der zur Ergreifung der Schuldigen führen kann, der nächsten deutschen oder französischen Polizeidienststelle zu geben.

Paris, am 10. Juli 1942.

Der Höhere SS- und Polizeiführer
Im Bereich des Militärbefehlshabers in Frankreich.

AVIS

Après avoir observé l'attitude de la population française en zone occupée, j'ai constaté que la majorité de la population continue à travailler dans le calme. On désapprouve les attentats, les actes de sabotage, etc. tramés par les Anglais et les Soviets dirigés contre l'armée d'occupation, et l'on sait que c'est uniquement la vie paisible de la population civile française qui en subirait les conséquences.

Je suis résolu a garantir d'une façon absolue, en pleine guerre à la population française la continuation de son travail dans le calme et la sécurité. Mais j'ai constaté que ce sont surtout les proches parents des auteurs d'attentat, des saboteurs et des fauteurs de troubles qui les ont aidés avant ou après le forfait. Je me suis donc décidé à frapper des peines les plus sévères non seulement les auteurs d'attentats, les saboteurs et les fauteurs de troubles eux-mêmes une fois arrêtés, mais aussi, en cas de fuite, aussitôt les noms des tuyards connus, les familles de ces criminels, s'ils ne se présentent pas dans les dix jours après le forfait à un service de police allemand ou français.

Par conséquent, j'annonce les peines suivantes:

1.) Tous les proches parents masculins en ligne ascendante et descendante ainsi que les beaux-frères et cousins à partir de 18 ans seront fusillés.

2.) Toutes les femmes du même degré de parenté seront condamnées aux travaux forcés.

3.) Tous les enfants, jusqu'à 17 ans révolus, des hommes et des femmes frappés par ces mesures seront remis à une maison d'éducation surveillée.

Donc, je fais appel à tous pour empêcher selon leurs moyens les attentats, les sabotages et le trouble et pour donner même la moindre indication utile aux autorités de la police allemande ou française afin d'appréhender les criminels.

Paris, le 10 juillet 1942.

Der Höhere SS- und Polizeiführer
Im Bereich des Militärbefehlshabers in Frankreich.

In response to increased Maquis activity, the Germans broadened the scope of their retaliatory

TRES SECRET   Mon cher ami,

La présence simultanée à Londres de
Bernard et de Charvet a permis d'établir
l'entente entre leurs deux mouvements de
résistance, et de fixer les conditions de leur
activité sous l'autorité du Comité National.

J'ai vivement regretté votre absence
pendant cette mise au point. Je pense, cependant,
que les dispositions qui ont été arrêtées
faciliteront l'exécution de la mission qui vous
est confiée.

Vous aurez à assurer la présidence du
comité de coordination au sein duquel seront
représentés les trois principaux mouvements de
résistance: "COMBAT", "FRANC-TIREUR", "LIBERATION".
Vous continuerez d'autre part comme représentant
du Comité National en zone non-occupée, à prendre

tous les contacts politiques que vous jugerez
opportuns. Vous pourrez y employer certains
de nos agents qui vous sont directement
subordonnés.

Toutes organisations de résistance,
quel que soit leur caractère, autres que les
trois grands mouvements groupés par le comité
de coordination, devront être invitées à affilier
leurs adhérents à l'un de ces mouvements et à
verser leurs groupes d'action dans les unités de
l'armée secrète en cours de constitution. Il
convient en effet d'éviter la prolifération de
multiples petites organisations qui risqueraient
de se gêner mutuellement, de susciter des
rivalités et de créer la confusion.

Je tiens à vous redire que vous avez
mon entière confiance et je vous adresse toutes
mes amitiés.

C. de Gaulle.

De Gaulle's letter creating a joint National Committee unifying the three principal resistance movements.

Jean Moulin. The scarf hides the scar from the wound in his neck.

Naval Lieutenant d'Estienne d'Orves.

Pierre Brossolette.

General Delestraint (Vidal).

Pierre Georges (Colonel Fabien).

Bertie Albrecht.

The link to the Allies: a radio transmitter hidden in a suitcase.

P.C.

GROUPEMENT CHABERT

VERCORS—CHAMBARAND—CHARTREUSE

HEAD QUARTIER

MAJOR CHABERT

Himmler, chief of the Gestapo, with Hitler on the Siegfried Line.

Joseph Darnand, the chief of Militia.

This photograph was distributed by the DNP with the following caption: "Members of the National French Socialist Militia struggle for a new Europe. In a recent action against terrorists in Brittany they took a number of prisoners, shown here. These men all have railroad sabotage, assassination and theft on their consciences. They have led themselves to a deserved punishment."

Railroad sabotage.

A member of the resistance whose hands were cut off by the Germans.

These resistance fighters are about to be executed.

November 11, 1943: Members of the FFI parade with their flag through the streets of Oyonnax.

Captain l'Herminier on the bridge of the Casabianca. The celebrated naval officer undertook countless missions to keep the resistance supplied with arms and ammunition.

Men of the Maquis close on Ajaccio. Corsica was the first department in France to be liberated.

The Maquis collects its supplies and buries parachutes.

A parachute supply drop from an American B-17.

The women kept the men of the Maquis supplied with food and other necessities.

COMITÉS DE LA LIBÉRATION
DE SEINE, SEINE ET OISE, SEINE-ET-MARNE
ORCES FRANÇAISES DE L'INTÉRIEUR

Ordre de Mobilisation Générale

ordre de mobilisation des officiers, sous-officiers dans les FFI, décrété par le Gouvernement Provisoire de la République Française, est étendu sur décision des Comités de la Libération et du Commandement des FFI de l'Ile-de-France à tous les français de 18 à 50 ans.

Comment s'enrôler dans les FFI ?

Dans chaque entreprise, rue, quartier, localité, arrondissement où les hommes visés par l'ordre de mobilisation doivent s'organiser :
- groupes de combat : (8 hommes qui désignent leur sergent chef de groupe) ;
- détachement : (4 groupes de combat) ;
- compagnie, en bataillons.

Armement

- er immédiatement toutes les armes stockées ou détenues, individuellement aux combattants.
- er leurs armes, par des attaques individuelles et des groupes de combat, aux Allemands et aux miliciens de Darnand.
- er les dépôts de l'ennemi, ses convois d'armes et de munitions.
- er des canons et des tanks, avec des unités spécialisées (tankistes, artilleurs, etc.)
- tous les moyens de fortune pour nuire à l'ennemi (armes blanches, grenades et bombes incendiaires, crève-pneus, câbles tendus, abattis d'arbres, cisailles liés à tire-fond, etc.)

FRANÇAIS, TOUS AU COMBAT

ponde à l'appel du Général de Gaulle en ouvrant la route de Paris aux armées alliées, en exterminant l'envahisseur, en hâtant par l'insurrection nationale la libération du pays.

COMITÉS DE LA LIBÉRATION
SEINE   SEINE-ET-OISE   SEINE-ET-MARNE

ord officiel des FFI

| FFI | Rouge |

Le Colonel Commandant les FFI
de Seine, Seine-et-Oise et Seine-et-Marne
Signé : ROL

The General Mobilization Order.

RÉPUBLIQUE FRANÇAISE

Liberté   -   Egalité   -   Fraternité

ARMEE   FRANÇAISE

F. F. I.   F.T.P.F.

ORDRE DE

MOBILISATION GENERALE

DES OFFICIERS ET SOUS-OFFIC... ...AIS

Le Gouvernement provisoire de la R... ... par
la voix du Général de GAUL... ...ous les
OFFICIERS, SOUS-OFFIC... ... Régiments
Bataillons, Compagnies, Dé... ...Régulière qui
se bat sur le sol de Fran... ...ent des ETATS-
MAJORS F.F.I. ... ...ens et traitres de Vichy.
... ...e de la République Française.

Nous vous avertissons! Pensez au sort de Paris.
DER WEHRMACHTBEFEHLSHABER VON PARIS.

AUX P... ...S A PORTER LES ARMES

...s de Parisiens abattent des Boches, des miliciens,
...es camions allemands, des garages, des usines travaillant
...uerre allemande. Des convois de Boches sont attaqués par
...pagnies Parisiennes :

...se ;	Vaillant-Couturier ;	Corentin-Quideau ;
...Héroïque ;	Les Détachements Barra ;	Saint-Just ;
Commune de Paris ;	Oradour-sur-Glanes (village de Haute-Vienne rasé par les S.S.)	De la Garde, etc...

Tous les hommes et femmes valides doivent rejoindre les rangs de l'Armée de
la France combattante et ses Milices Patriotiques.

...PELLE !
...CITOYENS !
...EZ VOS BATAILLONS !

Pour l'Etat-Major F.T.P.F.
Le Commandant.

The German commander picks up the order and issues it with his own warning: Think of the future of Paris.

Opposite—top: *Open insurrection in the streets of Paris. Three of the men in this picture are protecting themselves with captured German helmets.* Middle: *American soldiers watch as a party of resistance fighters marches off new prisoners.* Bottom: *German prisoners, guarded now by French gendarmes.*

The triumph of the resistance, August 26, 1944. General de Gaulle strides down the Champs Elysées from l'Etoile to the Place de la Concorde, applauded by a delirious crowd and surrounded by the generals of his armies, the ministers of the new provisional government, and members of the National Council of the Resistance.

promise that officers taken as hostages will be treated like French army prisoners of war."

"French army? You and your riff-raff?"

The conversation quickly took an ugly turn. After an angry exchange, Lefèvre seemed on the point of leaving. But he suddenly spun around, his pistol in his hand, and fired point blank at Tom Morel. Struck in the chest, the Glières leader fell. Lieutenant Humbert rushed to his side. Lefèvre was about to shoot him too but didn't have time: a burst of machine-gun fire cut him in two.

The doctor and his assistant carried Tom to a neighboring café which had been converted into a field aid station. Once there, they soon realized that the bullet had pierced Tom's heart and killed him instantly. Géo, a leader of the attack force, had also been killed. A few other members of the Maquis were slightly wounded, but one man, Frizon, suffered a serious face wound. Forty-seven G.M.R. were taken prisoner and transported to the plateau.

The bodies of Tom and Géo were brought as far as La Louvetière on sleds. Then the long climb began. By late afternoon, Tom was laid out in the infirmary under a sheet bearing the Cross of Lorraine. The room, hung with blue, white, and red parachutes, was transformed into a morgue.

The funeral services took place on March 13. Théodose Morel's parents were present. They had gone to see Colonel Lelong to request a pass. Lelong, claiming he was being watched too closely by the Germans, said he couldn't comply but advised them to talk to Abbé Truffy. The abbé managed to obtain from the local commander of the G.M.R. permission to cross the barricades in the company of the dead man's parents.

On that same day, Lelong sent Vichy notice of his resignation. But the tenor of the letter was known to the Germans even before it was sent, and the answer was not long in coming. Lelong was ordered to remain at his post and to participate wholeheartedly in any actions the Germans might deem necessary—

"after due consultation"—to eliminate the Haute-Savoie "terrorists."

A replacement for Tom Morel had to be found. Lieutenant Jourdan-Joubert, who served as interim commander, recalled this moment:

> I now felt the entire burden of Tom's cares and responsibilities—which he had borne so lightheartedly and magnificently—on my own shoulders. I realized then all that he had meant to us; he had managed to sort out the most confused situations with complete clarity and had performed on his own the work of three or four men. We longed for a leader competent enough to replace this irreplaceable man. I had asked Clair, the departmental chief, to send us Captain Anjot because he possessed both military experience and comprehensive knowledge of the organization that was working for us in the surrounding valleys. Thanks to a fortunate coincidence, Anjot decided quite spontaneously to come up and join us. Later we were able to appreciate the selflessness that had prompted his decision.

On March 19 Anjot arrived on the plateau. The mission he had assumed involved a sacrifice which he understood as well as the men he was to lead. The information brought by the brave liaison agents was crystal clear. The Maquis could no longer count on the help of people in the neighboring valleys, which hitherto had proved so effective, because of the dangers such help now entailed. The net was being drawn tighter with each passing day. This affected everyone's morale. Within a week, fourteen men had deserted.

German planes began their bombardment of Glières on March 12. Initially only three aircraft dropped bombs, and the damage was not serious—a few huts hit and several men slightly wounded and subsequently treated in the infirmary. But a second raid on March 17 was followed by expanding aerial operations.

At dawn on March 20 the militia launched a dual assault.

By nightfall, after an entire day of fierce fighting, the enemy was forced to fall back, leaving twelve men dead, their bodies streaking the snow with blood. Seven members of the Maquis were killed, three were wounded, and one was taken prisoner.

On March 22 Dagostini, commander of the militiamen who surrounded the plateau, had one of his men contact Canon Pasquier, head of the Catholic school in Thônes. Pasquier, told that large German detachments were soon to arrive, wished to see negotiations opened during the next several hours with the Glières commander, in order to avoid the worst.

A young priest, Abbé Gavel, whose brother belonged to the Maquis, was sent to Dagostini. The commander of the militia demanded nothing less than unconditional capitulation. His only concession was a promise to give more favorable treatment to those rebels whose past life had been "honest" and who had been "deceived" by British propaganda. He would "regularize" their status and free them, but they would have to perform obligatory labor service. As for the "terrorists," they would be handed over to French tribunals.

Abbé Gavel reported the results of this interview to Canon Pasquier and added that his primary mission was to transmit a message from Dagostini to the commander at Glières. The following day, the two priests climbed up to Anjot's headquarters.

The two priests visited all the platoons stationed on the plateau to offer the men their spiritual offices. Later Canon Pasquier had a private talk with Anjot, which he recalled afterwards: "After apprising Anjot of the large-scale preparations the Germans were making—at least insofar as I myself knew about them—I told him that from a purely military point of view, the position on the plateau would soon become untenable, that continuation of the struggle would lead to mass slaughter. I found him to be in complete agreement with me on this point. He knew, he said, that he himself would not survive. As a matter of fact, he was entirely reconciled to the idea of such a self-sacrifice.

"I stressed once again that he must think first of all of his men and of his responsibility to them. Accordingly, I advised him to try a face-to-face meeting with Dagostini, who had suggested it. As soon as I said this, I realized that he had been thinking about nothing else all afternoon. Instead of answering me like a soldier in the negative as he had done when I first arrived, he now spoke thoughtfully, like a leader who had weighed everything carefully and courageously assumed his responsibilities."

Anjot answered as follows: "You see, Monsieur Abbé, your suggestion of an interview is unacceptable because it would be useless and also harmful to the morale of my men. It would be useless, to begin with. Ever since the forces of law and order arrived in Haute-Savoie, we have had a number of direct or indirect contacts with Colonel Lelong and his officers. Even though they acknowledge, or at least so they say, our exclusively patriotic sentiments, and declare their readiness to distinguish between our cause and that of the so-called terrorists, they nonetheless continue to harass us, to push us back as far as they can, to cut off all our food supplies. Today they are grouping around this plateau; tomorrow we will become the easy prey of the enemy.

"The interview itself, which my officers and men would certainly be informed of, would damage their morale. They would sense some vacillation in my mind, and this would cause them, too, to hesitate. Now, at this critical juncture, having accepted the idea of sacrificing themselves, they require only one thing: steadfastness. I do not want to incur the responsibility of undermining it."

Canon Pasquier commented: "Anjot's point was well taken. He had expressed his views clearly and calmly, which was what I had hoped for. These Glières soldiers were about to make a magnificent sacrifice. They were accepting a difficult battle for the sake of their honor! Glières would come to symbolize something more than a victory; it would be a sign, a declaration of resistance to the oppressor, sealed in blood. I bowed to Captain Anjot and told him that I agreed with his views. My mission was completed."

The enemy forces began to take up their attack positions. Wehrmacht batteries, departing from Entremont, were en route to Petit-Bornand. One of them encountered the Maquis's machine-gun fire and suffered some losses. This was the first skirmish.

The neighboring Maquis tried to slow the German attack. At dawn on March 24 the railroad station at St.-Jean-de-Maurienne was blown up, delaying the transportation of one group. As a result, there was some thought of postponement, but the Germans, fearing that the terrorists had been ordered to leave the plateau one by one, decided to attack no later than March 26.

Anjot tried to play his last card. Via Captain Clair and with his approval, he sent a message to the regional F.T.P. commander in Lyon. He asked the Communists to help by dispatching a force of 2,000 men from Haute-Savoie. Thus reinforced, and bolstered by the parachuting of food supplies and munitions, he thought he would be able, as he stated in his letter, to contain a German attack, no matter how determined the enemy forces might be. He hoped to hold out until the time of the Allied landing. But he readily admitted that without such assistance the Maquis of the Secret Army faced certain defeat.

For three days no response arrived from Lyon. Then, a message to the F.T.P. units on the plateau ordered their immediate withdrawal.

But this order was only partially carried out. The spirit of camaraderie, together with the example set by Tom Morel, proved so powerful that only Lamouille's small group left shortly after the German attack began. Enjoying unheard-of luck, they managed to cross the enemy lines and leave the region.

Anjot asked the Allies to neutralize the fields from which the enemy bombers took off, but again his efforts proved futile.

He received no food supplies, even though not a single loaf of bread was left.

On March 24 the militia launched its first attack against the forward posts on the Auges hill held by the "Ebro" platoon. Taken by surprise, the two Spanish sentries proved extremely courageous. Wounded, Credor and Garcia were stretched out in the snow where they continued to fire, delaying the militia's advance until they died of their wounds. Their action alerted the men commanded by Captain Antonio and Lieutenant Jouglas (the "Leclerc" platoon), and they quickly took up their positions. After two hours of fighting, the militia hurriedly retreated, carrying off their wounded.

On March 25 German artillery stationed around the plateau went into action, and the shelling was to continue for an entire day. Lieutenant Pouget wrote:[3]

> The last huts of the Monthiévret sector were burned down and destroyed. An acute anxiety gripped the inhabitants of neighboring villages that were filled with soldiers in green uniforms. Bayard's men were fiercely determined. Their teeth clenched, they watched the destruction of their mountain homes. Soon their only shelter would be the snow.

At dawn on March 26 the militiamen attacked once more, this time from the west at Enclave and the Landron gorges, from the north through the Freux pass. Again they were pushed back, leaving behind twenty dead.

"Just a curtain-raiser," Anjot commented. They were waiting for the Germans and did not have long to wait. At ten in the morning the "Liberté Chérie" platoon, which was defending the left wing above the Spé pass, spotted a column of about forty men climbing up toward them. Sergeant Becker ordered the platoon to open fire, and noted the result:

---

3. *La France et son Empire dans la Guerre.*

"Six Boches were definitely hit. The rest took to the woods. But this minor success brought down upon us infernal machine-gun and cannon fire. We lay flat on our bellies until five o'clock."

The German attack was merely a diversion. The big assault came at eleven-thirty from the east against the Monthiévret position. The enemy's successes were in large part facilitated by information obtained from two G.M.R. prisoners who had managed to escape two days earlier. The "Sidi-Brahim" platoon in this area had to defend two sides of a rocky ridge overlooking the Borne valley. To get from one side to the other, the men had to cross exposed terrain around the ridge. As a result, each half of the platoon was isolated and unable to cover the area that would separate them in the event of an attack. After a few initial reconnoiters, the Germans had only to spread out fanwise and then encircle either of the posts in order to force a way through. And that is exactly what they did.

The eighteen men at the post near Entremont were overrun by waves of Germans totaling several hundred men and garbed in white so that they could scarcely be distinguished from the snow.

The German officer in charge halted his men near the post. "Resistance is useless," he shouted. "Give in."

"We'll be damned if we will!" replied the Maquis fighters.

From ten to three o'clock, in successive waves, Stukas set fire to the last huts, including the infirmary where the wounded were being evacuated to a shelter in the woods by Dr. Bombiger, who, himself wounded, would not leave the flaming building until he was sure all his patients were safe.

At noon one depot of explosives and another of ammunition were blown up almost simultaneously by German bombs.

An hour later, the militiamen were back in action. They renewed their attack at the Freux pass, held by about twenty men under Sergeant Buchet's command, and at Enclave-Landron, which was defended by Chief Adjutant Morel and a dozen maquisards. In spite of numerous assaults as well as intense artillery fire, Buchet remained in control of the situation. Morel, too, after several hours of successive attacks, managed to prevent the militia from gaining ground.

By nightfall the Monthiévret stronghold, although still in the hands of its defenders, was beginning to be overrun. The Spaniards stood, fought, and died. The Germans, advancing in successive waves and undeterred by their losses, headed toward the Lamotte headquarters. The *groupe-franc* of Thônes, under the command of "Chocolat" (André Guy), was encircled and its leader killed. The "Jean Carrier" platoon, led by Lieutenant Baratier, suffered the same fate. Lamotte's company was overrun.

The Germans infiltrated the plateau. They advanced very slowly in the dark, fearful of encountering reconnaissance forces. They did not know that such forces were nonexistent.

Anjot realized that the respite would be very short—until the following morning. He had no more reserves with which to establish a front line. To continue the struggle would be to doom his isolated men to quick and useless extermination. Around ten that night he talked with Jourdan-Joubert, explained the situation, and concluded:

"It seems to me that our honor has been saved."

"I think so too," Jourdan-Joubert replied.

Thereupon Anjot ordered a general retreat. Each platoon was to attempt to rejoin its original Maquis unit after withdrawing via Parmelan. However, the order arrived so late at the farthermost sectors that it could not be carried out. Each man fended for himself as best he could. Some, leaving for Entremont, went down to the Borne valley. Forty-three maquisards managed to cross the Freux pass and reach St.-Laurent or La Roche. Morel's platoon headed for Thorens and was able to get through the militia's barricade.

The group that went down toward Thônes with Anjot, Bastian and Jourdan-Joubert came upon an area closely patrolled by the Germans. It was a difficult march, as Julien Helfgott has testified:

> Little by little, fatigue overcame us. For some of the men, especially the weak and the wounded, every step was sheer agony. Jean Rivaud, hit during a bombardment and not yet recovered, his eyes burning with fever, walked with our support, a big smile lighting up his face but wincing at each step; he would stiffen and then continue the endless march. We had to cross the freezing waters of the Fier, which were swollen by melting snow. We hung on, clinging together by threes. Paul was carried away by the current, and we had a hard time retrieving him.
>
> But there was something more terrible than the physical fatigue—our lassitude. It threatened the patience we needed to take every essential precaution. Some of the men, indifferent to obvious risks, wanted to hasten their own deliverance. They were willing to take chances, to gamble. This was the attitude of Vitipon, who, after a short pause, suddenly made up his mind: "My papers are in order, I've got clean clothes to change into, I'll go straight to Annecy and link up with the others there. The Boches won't catch me." Unfortunately, a few hours later, he was killed at Nâves, alongside Captain Anjot and Duparc, head of the ski scouts, whom he had met on his way.
>
> Late in the evening, at Belle-Inconnue near Thônes, two ski scouts, Quétand and Sala, both valiant and daring men, moved ahead of us to clear the path we were to follow. We had a fixed meeting place, but we waited for them in vain. Their weapons in their hands, they were captured by a Boche patrol and shot on March 30 at Isle.

Helfgott's group was caught in an ambush in the Morette gorge:

> Firing broke out in front of us, the light of the fire illuminating a corner of the woods, giving us a glimpse of about fifty attacking Boches. We all hid. Some were never to rise again. Bedet slid down eight yards and was captured. Gaby disappeared behind a tree. We never saw him again.

The German machine-gun fire was intense. Of the twenty-five men in the group, only eight, miraculously spared, remained a few hours later.

More than 200 escapees were captured by the militia and the Germans. The punishment meted out was pitiless. Some were shot then and there. Thirteen of them were seen tied one behind the other, like animals in a butcher shop. Soon there was the sound of gunfire. The local mayor was ordered to toss the bodies into a ditch, to "muddy them up," to quote the phrase used by the German captain in charge.

But in spite of German threats, the mayor refused to bury the victims in such summary fashion. He had their bodies brought to the Morette gorge, at the foot of the Glières plateau. A separate grave was dug for each man, and each grave had its own cross. Thus originated the cemetery which today harbors a hundred heroes, all of whom fell in this first of the Resistance battles.

But the list of the victims was not complete. Bastian and Lalande were captured, tortured, then murdered by the Germans 100 yards from the Morette gorge. Bastian, whose condition was somewhat less terrible than that of his companion in misery, was forced to dig the ditch into which their bodies would be thrown. All in all, eighty-three Glières fighters were executed in like fashion. On March 26 forty-two died in combat during the retreat. Abbé Truffy was deported. Captain Clair's identity was discovered. His wife, who resided in Annecy under her real name, was deported, as were many other Haute-Savoie resisters.

The enemy, too, suffered heavy casualties. The Germans lost 700 men in combat, the militia 150. Siegel, a G.M.R. spy, was killed near the prison of Annecy by two F.T.P. men. After the liberation, Colonel Lelong was arrested in Paris. Transferred to Annecy to be tried, he was kidnapped by the F.T.P. on October 16 and murdered at a place called Beau-Rivage. This bit of summary revenge only brought dishonor to its perpetrators; and it was but one of many acts at the start of the civil warfare that needlessly cast a shadow over the liberation of France.

Although the Glières battalion constituted a symbol for the Resistance, it served the same purpose for the Vichy government. Laval wanted to prove to everyone that he could maintain law and order in his own fashion on French territory. This explains Colonel Lelong's efforts to obtain, one way or another, the surrender of the Glières Maquis. It also explains why Joseph Darnand committed so much military strength to Haute-Savoie, and why he himself supervised the operations there.

Philippe Henriot, in a broadcast from Annecy on March 29, declared, "I do not know how sadly I would view today's glorious sunset had I not glimpsed once again the admirable band of soldiers fighting for law and order against unworthy and cowardly adversaries."

In this odious and shocking commentary, Henriot was careful not to mention the fact that it was the Germans themselves who had undertaken to crush the resistance of the heroic Glières fighters.

~~~~~~~~

CHAPTER NINE

THE MONT-MOUCHET
BATTALION

SOUTH OF THE Saint-Flour road in Puy, about ten miles east of the famous Garabit viaduct, Mont-Mouchet is close to the heights of the Margeride hills. There, on May 27, 1944, 2,700 maquisards gathered. They were prepared to wage what was to become a veritable two-day battle against 11,000, then 15,000 Germans,[1] another of the extraordinary demonstrations of the armed strength and readiness for combat of the Resistance forces at this time.

The order for this massive deployment had been issued on May 20 by Colonel Coulaudon, code named Gaspard. Posted on the walls of the town hall, it read like a genuine order for general mobilization:

---

1. The main portions of this chapter have been taken from Colonel Gaspard's account in *La France et son Empire dans la Guerre*.

The army of liberation has now been established in the heart of our Auvergne mountains.

I am reminding the responsible leaders that, except for individuals who have been charged with specific missions (sabotage, purge, intelligence), all men without exception (sedentary persons as well as maquisards) must join us.

The defeatists will be eliminated from the Free French Force of Liberation.

Each man must bring with him his best pair of shoes or sabots; socks and underwear; one or two warm blankets; his weapons, if he has received any; and if possible, a tent or tarpaulin for ten men.

The head of each group must make sure that a truck will be available for transporting his men.

There is every reason to join up immediately before the roads are barricaded and the German plan (black lists) is put into operation.

> To the Maquis
> May 20, 1944
> Regional F.F.I. leader
> Gaspard.

N.B. Draw up a list of men whose departure may result in a request for assistance to family dependents.

Not everyone obeyed with blind enthusiasm. Some even tried to disqualify themselves as quickly as possible. The F.T.P. waited several weeks before joining.

At the time that Colonel Coulaudon (Gaspard) became involved in this enterprise, he was certain that Allied airlifts would lend decisive support to the Maquis on D-day. There was in fact something well founded in this belief, as Guillain de Bénouville has confirmed:[2]

During my last trip to Berne, the Allies asked me to study a plan for the creation of a national redoubt in France. On the

---

2. *Le Sacrifice du Matin.*

day of the Allied landing, it could serve both as a fortress from which the Resistance troops would take off and an enclosure where Allied planes arriving during the day could deliver the light and semi-heavy equipment we would need.

And later he noted:

A detailed plan had been drawn up by the D.G.S.S. [*Direction générale des Services spéciaux,* headed by Jacques Soustelle]. An organized supplementary force composed of specialized units was being readied. It was to be parachuted in and brought by gliders to our redoubt, where it would be positioned.

This special unit was called Force C. According to the code used at the time, Force A comprised French detachments that were to participate in the Allied landings in the northern zone; Force B was the cover name for units that would become part of General de Lattre's army when it disembarked in the southern zone. As it turned out, the Supreme Allied Command did not make use of Force C, but this was something the maquisards knew nothing about. When he issued his mobilization order, Gaspard did not yet know that he would never have airlifts to help him.

Three separate redoubts were contemplated by the Grand Council of the Auvergne Resistance. One was to be in the hills of Margeride, another near Haute-Lozère at Paulhac, and the third in the Lioran mountains. Colonel Gaspard set up his command post at Mont-Mouchet.

The units were dispersed as follows: the 5th, 6th, and 7th companies of Captains Antoine Alizon, Marquis, and Paul Coupat (Guignet battalion) patrolled the roads in the north and northeast. The 4th was stationed close to Ruynes and Clavières, while the 10th and 14th patrolled the Pinols sector and the Langeac highway.

In the south, the 2nd and 11th companies were in the environs of Paulhac-en-Margeride, where the road from St.-Chely-d'Apcher began. The 3rd (Captain Marcel) held the heights above Lorcières and Clavières. The 12th company and the Laurent *corps-franc,* stationed outside the redoubt at Chamlard, joined the Haute-Loire units commanded by Gevold in holding the highways extending from Langeac and Puy.

On June 2, 800 S.S. men, rushed to the scene from Mende, opened the German attack. They had orders to "clear" Mont-Mouchet.

At 7:00 A.M. the 2nd company (Captain Eloi, Lieutenant Jouanneau) absorbed the initial thrust. Then, for three hours, it sustained an attack launched from Paulhac, supported by mortar fire and automatic weapons.

The Germans were attempting to overrun the local forces of the Maquis. They came up against the Truands *corps franc* (Lieutenant Danton) dispatched by Commander Judex to the neighboring heights[3] and were forced to retreat. Their right flank was in serious trouble, blocked by the 3rd and 11th companies (Captains Marcel and Lavenue), which counterattacked.

Back at the command post, Colonel Garcie lost no time. He ordered Commander Laurent, who was at the château of Chamblard, to attack the German flank, with the support of the 12th company (Captain Samama). One of Samama's platoons was charged with the task of providing cover in the eastern sector.

The *corps-franc* and the men of the 12th company immediately took up positions at the entrance to the woods, harassing the enemy with machine-gun fire. Already worn out and de-

---

3. The historian Robert Aron has written the following about the "Truands": "Born scrappers, they had already become legendary. It was said of them, although without too much supporting evidence, that they practised a policy of sharing their wealth and their women, especially women prisoners. It was also said that to be initiated into their ranks, a man had to undergo a baptism that consisted of downing three-quarters of a liter of red wine, three-quarters of a liter of white wine, and three-quarters of a liter of hooch. After which, properly fortified, he could be considered ready to enter the fray."

moralized, the Germans took to their heels, rushing to fling themselves into trucks which were already piled high with dead and wounded men. The attackers had suffered a serious setback.

At the time, Colonel Gaspard wrote:

> From June 2 to June 10 our days will be hectic. We will take advantage of the respite the enemy has given us to reinforce our positions.
>
> The bridges and roads are mined, shelters are being prepared or improved, and the region is being purged of the spies and militiamen who have overrun the place. A military court is sitting; it is severe but just. Its verdict cannot be appealed.
>
> We no longer receive any volunteers here. Captain Pireyre is directing them from the Maquis retreat in Vins-Haut, which comprises the redoubt adjacent to La Truyère, where 1,500 men have assembled, and also the one at Saint-Genès, where Commander Mabrut has collected more than 2,000 men and will soon have 6,000. Unfortunately, we will not be able to arm all these people for several weeks. If we include the 800 armed lads at Haute-Loire who are billeted east of the local redoubt, our forces will total no more than 10,000 combat-ready men in this part of the Massif Central.

At that time, as General von Runstedt's daily reports show, the clandestine activity in the Massif Central was a great anxiety to the Germans. The general's memorandum of June 5 reads: "In the Clermont-Ferrand region, members of the Secret Army appear in public for the first time in uniform, wearing the tricolor cockade. We are preparing countermeasures . . ."

Powerful military forces were being pressed into service. For example, 1,500 German trucks were seen around Lioran and Murat, and several hundred more near Le Puy and Brioude. Reconnaissance planes were constantly flying over the Mont-Mouchet region.

The local branch of the Maquis felt confident. Allied parachute drops increased. The commandos were waging incessant guerrilla warfare. At the Lempdes bridge, Laurent gave the enemy a hard fight, and the Truands did likewise at Murat.

Then, on June 5, the men who listened to the famous broadcasts signaling D-day were overcome with enthusiasm.

"The landing is scheduled for tomorrow!" one of them shouted. He had just heard two messages: "His suit is billiard-colored" and "What does crab-apple have to say?" They had already heard: "The kick-off will take place at three o'clock." This had not been countermanded. Otherwise the men would have been told: "Put away your bayonets."

Gaspard wrote:

> If we are on the eve of the big fight, at least we know that our efforts will be coordinated with those from the outside. We will have to hold firm and not yield an inch of terrain if we wish to preserve the integrity of our groups. They will have to keep on fighting until all our territory has been liberated.

On June 6 the game was played out on the Normandy beaches. Airlifted units were being used behind the lines of the new front. But nothing reached the Auvergne redoubts save the usual matériel dropped by parachute.

At dawn on June 10 the Germans launched a strong attack against the Mont-Mouchet positions. Cannon thundered in the northern and southeastern sectors.

Colonels Gaspard and Prince visited the front line manned by the 3rd company (Captain Marcel). Gaspard noted:

> It was easy for us to observe everything through our field glasses. An enemy column that looked very long to us seemed to halt in front of Clavières, which began to go up in flames. The men of the 4th company [Captain Hoche] were holding firm. And higher up, both the 3rd company and the 9th [Captain Yves] were preparing for any eventuality in case our front line was pierced.

Against fifteen companies and three *corps-franc* groups (Laurent, Judex, Eloi) the Germans pitted 8,000 men but later brought up reinforcements.

One platoon of the 7th company was positioned in trenches dug by the men all along the road leading to the national highway at Moulergue. Here it could dominate the approaches to Chambon. The sound of 75s and mortars grew louder.[4]

During the night a liaison agent of the Moulergue group came to tell the platoon lieutenant: "The American commander has just left Moulergue. The entire F.T.P. team of parachutists has done likewise. Your order is to fall back. Try to save the supplies we are leaving behind."

What had happened in the redoubt that led to this decision? In the Ruynes sector, German armored cars had advanced a little, paying dearly as they did so. By early afternoon the lead machine gun had been put out of commission by a bazooka rocket from the 9th company's front line. Because the German infantry was unable to follow, the armored cars were gradually isolated, then partly encircled by motorized units.

At La Laubie, four miles southeast of Ruynes, Captain Marcel had pushed back the German infantry and Captain Hoche had caught them in the rear from the excellent positions his company occupied at Morte and Machot.

Finally, above Clavières, the enemy had been unable to break through the tight net formed by three companies (Hoche, Marcel, Yves). The column had turned around but before doing so had set fire to Clavières, Lorcières, and a number of isolated farms. At Ruynes the Germans took their revenge on the inhabitants. Twenty-seven men were shot in the presence of women and children.

Nine members of the Maquis enrolled in the 3rd company were encircled, captured, and felled by bullets in the neck. Yet

---

4. Based on the account authored by Joseph-Louis Sanciaume.

all of them were in uniform and wore arm bands bearing the Cross of Lorraine.

The attack from the east and the southeast had been contained by Judex's Truands. But Lieutenant Fred and some twenty of his men who had refused to yield met death in the course of a heroic battle.

"Their sacrifice was not in vain," wrote Colonel Gaspard. "The delay of several hours which they forced upon the foe allowed the 10th and 14th companies, for whom Captain Laboureur, Lieutenant Camille Vacant, and Captain Bertrand were performing heroically, to block the enemy's advance until late in the afternoon. This brought us victory by the end of the day."

Elsewhere, at Monistrol, the Germans had to abandon two cannon and one armored car, leaving many of their dead on the field. At Pinols, unable to break through, they fell back at nightfall, fearful—quite justifiably—that the maquisards would take advantage of the dark to launch a counterattack.

Gaspard noted:

> Despite the successful employment of our weapons, we must envisage the possibility of a battle that will last several days, during which the enemy is bound to bring up reinforcements.
>
> Thanks to the resistance they encountered at Pinols and Monistrol, the Germans were obliged to leave the southern route open [La Croix-du-Fau, Le Malzieu]. We decided to remove during the night all our rolling stock, food reserves, and clothing and to head for the Truyère redoubt. This would enable us, in case we were intercepted, to move through the woods without further losses.

At dawn on June 11 the command post learned that 200 trucks had been seen leaving Clermont the night before. They were transporting 4,000 to 5,000 men.

Nine o'clock: machine-gun and cannon fire resumed near Clavières and evoked a lively response. Above the Pinols crossroads, the Germans clashed with the 14th company, which inflicted heavy losses on the enemy. Everywhere the units involved fought fiercely. But the shortage of supplies forced them to use their ammunition sparingly. The order went out to hold firm until nightfall because it was impossible to escape during the day. The command was planning an evacuation at 10:00 P.M.

At the appointed hour, the maquisards fell back in good order. The ordeal seemed endless, as Joseph-Louis Sanciaume, recalling the 7th company's retreat, has recounted:

> Over hill and dale, through the gorse, the convoy moved slowly. The men carried their personal belongings. Guns and ammunition had been divided up among all of them. Noiselessly, listening for every sound, every rustle in the night, they marched, their minds filled with one thought alone.
>
> About three in the morning they halted. A little bread and some springwater appeased the men's hunger pangs. They were in a village called Faverolles. Its inhabitants had taken their bedding into the woods and slept there, living in a state of perpetual alert.

The night passed without incident. Throughout the following day, the men remained hidden in the woods. Observation planes, the "stool pigeons," flew constantly over the area but, finding no sign of life, finally disappeared. The men then marched on, heading toward Chaudes-Aigues.

But their troubles were not yet over. They had to cross the gorges of Truyère. On the morning of the second day, they reached Mallet. No food was to be had there since several thousand men had gone through the village the day before. The peasants had given all they could spare. On the third day, trucks finally arrived to pick up the men, and they were transported to Paulhac without incident.

The Mont-Mouchet affair cost the Germans 1,400 dead and 1,700 wounded. Gaspard noted: "Among our men, the Truands' *corps-franc,* Colonel Thomas's battalion, and the 3rd and 14th companies were the hardest hit. We counted approximately 160 dead and 100 wounded."

At Saint-Martial, where Gaspard installed his new command post, an impressive parade took place on June 18 to commemorate the fourth anniversary of de Gaulle's appeal from London.

Henri Ingrand, representing the Republic, delivered his first public address. Then Gaspard declared: "Soon we will go down to the cities, and the death of our comrades will be avenged by the liberation of our country and the irretrievable defeat of Germany's forces."

Then it was the turn of the F.F.I. to file by. Gaspard described the scene:

A Truands platoon came forward, marching in step. That day even the toughest men made no effort to disguise their emotions. In the Mont-Mouchet battle they had lost some of their first comrades: Danton, Spada, Fred. These men had held out in order to slow the German advance and enable the others to get away. They were killed on the spot. As the troops filed by, a German plane flew over the village and its gunner unleashed a volley of shots—a reminder that the danger was not yet over.

On June 19 the local leaders, misinterpreting the instructions or messages broadcast over the BBC, issued mobilization orders. Young people flocked in to Saint-Martial. Obviously, they had had no training whatsoever. Gaspard had no difficulty organizing three additional companies, but they were of mediocre quality.

The region was crowded with German troops. They could be seen everywhere. On June 20, as the cannon thundered, 20,000 men, supported by tanks and planes, launched a fresh attack against 4,000 maquisards who had only light weapons with which to defend themselves.

The 7th company endured the brunt of the assault. Enemy

forces came at them from St.-Chely-d'Apcher, passing through Fournels. But they encountered vigorous resistance at St.-Juery. Additional enemy troops attacked the Mallet bridge in Fridefont. Chaudes-Aigues too was in danger, and it looked as if the entire redoubt might be encircled. But at this point the plans for widespread sabotage came into play, and several bridges were at once blown up.

The 7th company resisted until nightfall. This afforded a much-needed respite. At 10:00 P.M. Colonel Gaspard and his chief of staff in the command post at Saint-Martial decided in favor of another retreat, this time to the Lioran mountains. The orders were transmitted to liaison agents.

Taking advantage of the darkness, the men in charge of the evacuation carried out their mission without incurring heavy losses, save for one tragic episode: eighty-five wounded maquisards, eighteen of them in critical condition, sought refuge in the woods. They had not an ounce of strength left. And it was a Frenchman who, in exchange for a sizable sum, led the Germans to their hiding place. Most of the wounded managed to escape, but nine of the critically injured, unable to move, were massacred on the spot.

Colonel Gaspard and his men had been victimized by the myth of that Force C, an entity which in fact never existed. They learned their lesson from these events. From then on, the F.F.I. of Auvergne, making no further attempt to wage open warfare, engaged exclusively in guerrilla action.

~~~~~~~~

CHAPTER TEN

MAQUISARDS
AND PARACHUTISTS
AT SAINT-MARCEL

F ROM NOVEMBER 1943 to January 1944 the parachuting of
weapons ceased almost entirely because of bad weather, but
it increased considerably throughout France during the spring
of 1944, as D-Day approached.

Jacques Soustelle has noted:

> By the start of April we had parachuted 117,000 grenades,
> 72,000 machine pistols and rifles, 3,300 heavy Bren or Vickers
> machine guns, 138 mortars, about 500 anti-tank guns, including
> some American bazookas, and—I need hardly add—countless
> plastic bombs and much sabotage matériel.

But what was happening to weapons on the ground? The
commander-in-chief of the F.T.P., Charles Tillon, complained
bitterly about the way in which this matériel was being distributed. At the end of May 1944 the F.T.P.'s Military Committee

dispatched a statement to all Resistance newspapers charging that it was not receiving any weapons at all from the C.F.L.N. military authorities.

It was entirely possible that certain regional military delegates were leery of the F.T.P. and wondered—not without good reason—whether, once France was liberated, weapons given to it might not serve political ends quite unrelated to the clearly defined task of combating the nation's enemy.

In reality, however, it seems that an appreciable quantity of arms was delivered to the F.T.P. They were also given plenty of money, which enabled them to accumulate a comfortable amount not only for their war treasury but also for use in time of peace.

Those in high places were not eager, naturally, to have any weapons used too soon and possibly for conflicting purposes. General de Gaulle himself wrote:[1]

> The Allied Command . . . foresaw a prolonged battle and hoped that the Resistance would not precipitate matters except in the bridgehead area. The proclamation General Eisenhower read on the radio June 6 warned French patriots to stay on their guard. On the same day, however, I urged them to fight with all the means in their power according to the orders given by the French Command. But the delivery of arms depended on Allied headquarters and remained, at the start, limited. It was especially with regard to demolition of railways, roads, and essential communications that the Combined General Staff was concerned.

Increasingly the problem was to coordinate closely the operations of the French Resistance with those of the landing forces. The latter, moreover, needed tactical information that could be put to immediate use. To this end, a hundred liaison teams, called "Jedburghs," were trained, then parachuted into occupied territory. Each team consisted of two officers and a radio ser-

---

1. *War Memoirs,* Vol. II, p. 282.

geant, French or American. To collect the information garnered by these teams, a special air squadron was created to fly at night over their action zones.

The Americans were to send "Operational Groups" of thirty-two men each whose special mission it was to protect or destroy, as the case might be. Having done so, they were to join the nearest F.F.I. units and fight at their side.

There was also the Special Air Service (S.A.S.), an organization formed in Egypt in 1941 with the initial mission of dropping personnel behind enemy lines. French members of the S.A.S. brought off important coups in the Middle East, in Crete, and in Tunis, and then survivors of their group formed a unit in England known as the Second Parachute Regiment. This regiment, under the command of Colonel Bourgoin, was to be the first unit of the Free French Fighting Forces to set foot on French soil. Immediately after D-day, its primary task was to cut off all railway, road, and telephonic communications between Brittany and the rest of France, and thereafter it was to organize the Maquis in the Côtes du Nord and Morbihan departments.

In 1941 the Resistance in the Morbihan was largely inspired by Commander Guillaudot, head of the police and of the "Action" network. Most of the police brigade followed his lead, and this helped to endow the movement with a framework and a solid military structure.

During the first six months of 1943 twenty-nine parachute drops were received. By August 1943 volunteers were being trained in the use of weapons. On December 10 Guillaudot was arrested. Lieutenant-Colonel Morice immediately replaced him as head of the "Action" network. Soon after, General Audibert, commander of the Secret Army in the west, appointed Morice departmental commander. By this time, the forces in the area totaled 3,500 men, but their weapons were insufficient—400 Sten guns, 200 rifles, 150 pistols, 4,000 grenades, and nine tons of explosives. Nonetheless, by January 1944 each unit had its own *corps-franc.*

In February the movement suffered a serious blow. A departmental agent, captured by the Gestapo, revealed certain se-
crets under torture. This led to the arrest of General Audibert
Morice barely managed to escape the trap set for him.

An official report of June 1944 provided the following information about the composition of the local forces: ten F.T.P
battalions and nine Secret Army battalions. It was difficult, however, to make an exact comparison between the F.T.P. and the
Secret Army forces, because the number of men in each battalion
varied greatly—400 to 1,200. Besides, there was no watertigh
division between the two.

On June 4 the BBC broadcast the anticipated messages: guerrilla warfare and previously planned acts of sabotage were to
begin immediately. Lieutenant-Colonel Morice ordered a gen
eral mobilization. At the time, Morbihan could count on 12,000
members of the F.F.I. But there were also 10,000 men in the
Finistère, 10,000 in the Côtes du Nord, and 5,000 in Ille-et
Vilaine.

The red berets of the Second Parachute Regiment joined the
regional forces. The first phase of the parachute operations began on the night of June 5–6. Four groups, consisting of one
officer and seven noncommissioned officers and privates, served
as vanguards. The first groups, commanded by Lieutenants Bo
tella and Deschamps, were dropped over the Côtes du Nord to
establish a northern base dubbed "Samwest"; the other two
groups, commanded by Lieutenants Marienne and Deplante
were to set up a southern base in the Morbihan, code named
"Dingson."

Shortly after 11:00 P.M. Lieutenant Marienne's men were
assembling near the Plemelec windmill when they heard voice:
in the night. A man from Lorraine who spoke fluent German
reassured his companions: "Those aren't Germans."

"They're not speaking the Breton dialect either," another
said.

Gunfire broke out in every direction. The parachutists fired back, dispersed, and met again at a prearranged spot. One man, Corporal Bouétard, did not answer the roll call. He had fallen victim to a detachment of Russians in the pay of the German army. This sailor from Pleudihen in Brittany, who had enlisted in the F.F.I., was the first to die on the field of honor for the liberation of continental France.

Marienne and Deplante immediately sought contact with the Resistance. An observer recalled the occasion:[2]

> The resister Morizur greeted the parachutists and guided them in their search for a suitable base. They found it on the heaths of Lanvaux, near Saint-Marcel. The command post was set up in an isolated farmhouse at Le Nouët.
>
> Everyone quickly learned of the parachutists' arrival. The Resistance leaders came first to establish contact, and then hundreds of volunteers followed, all of them burning to fight.

Marienne was delighted. He delivered his first radio broadcast to Colonel Bourgoin: "Pierre I-station identification 101. Confirm message addressed by F.F.I. commander. Ten companies out of twenty-five very inadequately armed. Urgently request you send available officers, troops, and matériel, especially Bren guns. Your presence here is indispensable. Urgent. Am delighted by the organization and tremendous possibilities. Resistance command is certain it can aid Samwest from here. Charlotte and Dudule reconnoitered. Will be firmly installed and defended."

With the Normandy landings under way, the parachutists whose mission was sabotage went into action. Very quickly all the trains ceased to run, with the exception of the one from Brest to Rennes. Here a few convoys advanced slowly and with great difficulty. It took one train eighteen days to travel from Brest to Redon. Finally, an R.A.F. raid, unleashing bombs and torpedoes, put it out of commission.

---

2. Quoted by Yves Gwened in *La Liberté du Morbihan*.

One of the greatest acts of sabotage was accomplished during the night of June 7–8 by Lieutenant Camaret. His assignment was to cause a derailment in the Cobinière tunnel near Langon. To make sure that the tunnel would be obstructed, the parachutists, after blowing up some of the tracks, got hold of an old locomotive known as the "Pacific" which was stored in the depot. With the help of railroad employees, they started it off down the tracks. It entered the tunnel and emerged miraculously, without being derailed. But a German train proceeding on a different track proved less fortunate. Transformed into a heap of twisted iron, the train provided the best kind of obstruction. To make sure things were done properly, the parachutists returned three days later and blew up 900 more feet of the track to prevent the arrival of emergency equipment.

In Brittany, as in every other part of the country, repression was not the work of Germans alone. There the Germans made use of a gang that will be remembered by the sinister name of the "Perrot" militia. It was an offshoot of the Breton Nationalist Party,[3] a small separatist and Fascist group whose leaders had moved to Berlin in 1939. Named after a French priest killed by resisters for making Germanophile remarks, the Perrot militia had about a hundred members, all of whom sported the German uniform.

It was merciless. On June 10, after a clash with maquisards, it captured four resisters, among them Albert Tregaro, a sixteen-year-old. The men were imprisoned at Saint-Marcel. At first they were chained together on top of a pile of manure, then taken ten miles away to Saint-Martin-sur-Oust where the militia were quartered. Here they were tortured and shot.

The parachutists' northern base, "Samwest," was set up near Duault, southwest of Saint-Brieuc. Here, too, Lieutenants Botella and Deschamps were welcomed by the resisters. But the Germans reacted sharply, seizing hostages. On June 12 sixty German

---

3. Details given by J. Delperrie de Bayac in his *Histoire de la Milice.*

soldiers, who were reconnoitering the woods at Duault, came upon the Ker Hamon farm, where they discovered four parachutists and two maquisards. Determined to resist capture, the six men immediately opened fire. After a half hour of fierce combat, the Germans overcame them and set fire to the farm.

Botella, accompanied by seven parachutists and a maquisard, tried to ambush the Germans at the edge of the woods. German reinforcements totaling 100 men had just arrived. The scuffle turned out to be a wholesale slaughter of the Germans, because half a dozen parachutists were lying in wait for the enemy near the Saint-Servais road. At 1:30 P.M. the Ker Hamon farm was recaptured and the six prisoners freed.

At this point, Captain Leblond, commander of the "Samwest" base, decided to evacuate this northern redoubt and retreat to Saint-Marcel. Gradually the camp emptied out. Around 4:00 P.M. 300 Germans arrived in the vicinity of Ker Hamon. They split into two groups, each advancing cautiously. Circling the woods, they met in the midst of a glade, having seen and heard nothing. Midshipman Metz and his men, plus a dozen parachutists, chose this moment to open fire. Taken by surprise, the Germans withdrew in haste, with heavy losses.

Meanwhile, "Dingson," the southern base, was organizing. Little by little, after the sabotage commandos had completed their missions and returned to this redoubt, they joined the F.F.I. companies to swell their numbers and to assist in training them.

To the resisters pouring in, sometimes from great distances, the scene was impressive, as Briac Le Diouron (Commander Yacco) has attested:[4]

> It was about 4:30 P.M. [June 12] when we arrived at the village of Saint-Mathurin, about six miles from the Maquis camp. The impression made upon us by the build-up here was inspiring. We ascertained that the entire region was controlled by the F.F.I.

---

4. *Soldats de l'Ombre.*

We entered a café to quench our thirst and ask for information. While we were talking to the owner of the café, a group of maquisards appeared, their guns at the ready. They asked us who we were and where we were going. I introduced myself: "A member of the Maquis from the Loire-Inférieure department." Without further ado, they handcuffed us, loaded us into their car, and drove over the heathlands and through the pine forest.

It was an extraordinary spectacle: hundreds of armed men wearing bands on their sleeves instead of uniforms; vehicles, an infirmary, and the tricolor flag flying in the breeze . . .

Matters were quickly settled. The new arrivals' authenticity was soon verified.

Every night the R.A.F. flew over to drop weapons. By June 10 almost all the men of the Second Parachute Regiment were in Brittany, and so was their leader, Colonel Bourgoin, whose arrival was announced over the BBC with the jaunty message, "To all Pierres: the one-armed man has arrived safely." For this exceptional Frenchman the British had fashioned a huge tricolor parachute, which further underscored the spectacular nature of his arrival.

Bourgoin, who had lost an arm in the battle for Tunisia, was indeed present, his tall figure towering over the men. Reputedly an excellent game hunter before the war, he was quite at home in guerrilla operations. He set up his command post at Le Nouët, where Lieutenant-Colonel Morice and his principal adjutants were soon to join him.

The biggest parachute drop occurred on the night of June 17: 640 containers. Simultaneously, Lieutenant de la Grandière was dropped with a particularly well equipped team. Four jeeps were parachuted in and placed at his disposal. Twin Vickers machine guns were dropped in separate containers for mounting on each of the jeeps. The machine guns had reached the ground in sorry state because of the failure of the parachutes to open, but Sergeant Le Gall, an excellent gunsmith, somehow managed to rebuild one of each pair with the scattered pieces of both.

This parachute drop was marked by an incident that was to have important consequences. Five of the pilots, spotting lights, took them for the dropping-zone air strip. So they loosed their containers. Unfortunately, what they had seen were the lights of Roc Saint-André, four or five miles south of Saint-Marcel, where a German regiment was about to entrain.

An alarm was sounded. The next day, two cars containing German policemen accidentally took a road that led to La Nouët. A shell took care of the first car. The four occupants of the second car tried to flee. Three were killed, but the fourth escaped at the very moment when the priest of Saint-Marcel was celebrating mass under a canopy made of parachutes. He ended his sermon with these words:[5]

"We must speak not of vengeance, but of retaliation. They have won the first round, but with God's help we'll win the second. Let us prepare for combat . . ."

The battle of Saint-Marcel was about to begin. Morbihan's 2nd F.F.I. battalion, under the command of Lieutenant-Colonel Le Garrec, was charged with protecting the camp and the Le Nouët command post.[6] The 3rd company (Captain Cosquer) took up positions east of the plateau and south of Les Hardys-Behellec château. The 1st company (Captain Bessières) was installed west of the latter, about 600 yards from the abbey, while the 2nd company, posted north of the 3rd, covered the hamlet of Grands-Points. To its left it was linked with the 12th F.F.I. battalion (General de la Morlaye).

Early in the morning, the Germans attacked in force. By 9:15 they had captured the farm at Bois-Joly, but their main thrust was directed against the château. No doubt they thought it housed the command post.

The enemy's pressure increased from hour to hour. Several

---

5. Lieutenant Henry Corta, *Les Beréts Rouges*.
6. According to Lieutenant-Colonel Le Garrec's account in *La France et son Empire dans la Guerre*.

parachutists and maquisards were killed or wounded. Lieutenant Marienne was wounded, went to the first aid station at
the château for treatment, and then returned to the front lines.
He was everywhere, continuously riding up and down the lines
in his jeep, encouraging the men, helping them, fighting without
letup.

In answer to an appeal from Colonel Bourgoin, the R.A.F.
appeared around 4:00 P.M., harassing the enemy with rapid-fire
heavy bombing. Although most useful, their support did not
suffice. The Germans intensified their pressure. Concealed behind trees, their best riflemen felled the maquisards one by one.
Intelligence services operating in the surrounding hamlets alerted
Bourgoin to the arrival of numerous convoys and motorcyclists
as well as artillery reinforcements.

The French had to stand and fight as long as possible in
order to be able to fall back under the best possible conditions.
The commander decided to abandon the camp around 8:30 P.M.
and instructed his men to attempt to regroup in the Callac woods.

Lieutenant-Colonel Le Garrec has furnished some of the
details of the battle:

> Toward the end of the afternoon, the enemy, impatient to
> leave, intensified his fire. At six, as the firing increased, numerous
> German units arriving from the national highway attacked the
> 3rd company of the 2nd F.F.I. battalion. At 7:00 P.M. a battle
> was raging on the front held by our two units. Using incendiary
> bombs, the Germans set fire to the woods behind our lines. Liai-
> son with the camp, where final plans for withdrawal were being
> mapped out, became extremely difficult.
>
> The enemy, attacking in full force, clashed with our troops,
> but they did not budge. Machine-gun fire and flame throwers
> literally mowed down the Germans as they advanced through the
> wheat fields. Having suffered heavy losses, they were forced to
> regroup before resuming the attack. Our machine guns, carefully
> positioned, had a clear line of fire and repeatedly freed groups of
> our men just as they were about to be encircled. It was then 7:30

South of the camp, however, the Germans did succeed in getting very close to the F.F.I.'s lines. Lieutenant Rio, leading his platoon, forced the enemy back by tossing grenades until he himself succumbed to bullet wounds.

To enable the front-line fighters to withdraw, Lieutenant Félix Guillas, who headed a group of *corps-franc,* launched a counterattack. Simultaneously, the paratroopers went into action. Henry Corta has described the outcome of these synchronized thrusts:

> The enemy had his hands full because of powerful assaults led by Marienne, Taylor, La Grandière, Camaret, Lesecq, Tisné, and Brès—all seasoned parachutists or experienced maquisards to whom the invader was anathema.
>
> When night fell, we were at the edge of Saint-Marcel. We had gained almost two miles in one big thrust.

But no useful purpose would be served by seizing the village. The men withdrew to the posts they had held that morning. It was darker than usual for that time of night, and in addition it was raining, which wasn't a bad thing. All the matériel had been removed, except for munitions and explosives stored in two four-ton trucks.

Captain Puech-Samson remained with a handful of men. He made a tour of all the posts to make sure that everyone had left. Then he set the trucks on fire and blew them up.

The Rio group of LeGarrec's battalion was still in position to the right of the Les Hardys-Behellec château. The men heard the explosion. One of them has recounted:[7]

> After an instant of stupefaction for both ourselves and the enemy, who began yelling, we waited, not knowing what to do, our nerves taut, our hands clutching our weapons, holding our breath. We were only a few yards away from the enemy.

---

7. "Liberté du Morbihan," June 19, 1964.

After first checking on the exact position of the enemy, the parachutist, Calliou, warned us that we would have to attempt to get out before sunrise. We waited. For more than four hours we were trapped like animals in the dark night. Then we began to emerge, advancing singly, creeping along noiselessly in order to reach the Saint-Marcel highway leading to the abbey by 7:00 A.M.

Everyone seemed to be sleeping—not a sound, nothing stirring. Although we could just see the Le Nouët farm, we still had to cross the highway to reach the sheltered path leading to the command post. Quickened by the hope of rejoining our leaders and comrades, we started to cross the highway but were spotted by the enemy. A machine gun began firing at us from the direction of a village called Grands-Points-Les Hardys.

Eight o'clock. We reached the Le Nouët farm. Not a soul was there. Total discouragement and anguish. . . . The buildings were abandoned, weapons strewn around in disorder amid gaping suitcases. The sorry spectacle indicated a hurried flight during the night. We stared at each other, disappointed, exhausted, and hungry, no longer worrying about the danger nor about our enemies, who had not left their newly acquired positions.

So we were alone. We couldn't stay on in this sad place. We walked straight ahead, no longer taking precautions, indifferent weary, famished . . .

Noon. We glimpsed a village, Launay-Grippon, and approached it distrustfully; but the people were good, and we'll always remember how they welcomed us. Once our hunger was appeased, we hid in an attic, yearning for only one thing: sleep.

At 8:00 P.M. we were awakened. Liaison agents were looking for parachutists to regroup them and steer them toward Callac where they would join Lieutenant Marienne. Our two S.A.S. [Special Air Service] friends, our fellow fighters, the best men among us, were about to leave. We resigned ourselves as best we could and spent the night in this place, for the rain was pouring down.

They finally rejoined other Resistance groups. Lieutenant Corta noted:

From Callac a general dispersion took place. All the members of the F.F.I. went home, hid their weapons, and remained in contact with us. Those who had no home to go to followed the S.A.S. and joined small groups of maquisards that were forming here and there.

Meanwhile, the orders were plain: "Keep quiet and hide for two weeks or so. Afterward we will resume our work of sabotage."

General de Gaulle observed in his *War Memoirs:*

The news of the battle of Saint-Marcel managed to rouse all of Brittany. The invader found himself blockaded in the larger cities and the ports. . . . When Patton's armored units, having crossed the Avranches gap, debouched into Brittany at the beginning of August, they found the country entirely occupied by our men, who had already buried 1,800 German corpses and taken 3,000 prisoners.

CHAPTER ELEVEN

IN THE
BLOOD-SOAKED
WAKE OF THE
"DAS REICH" DIVISION

WITH THE INTENSIFICATION of Resistance activities in 1944, Hitler's forces in France resorted to ever more savage reprisals. The oldest S.S. unit, the 2nd Panzer Division, known as "Das Reich," was stationed in the Agen-Caussade-Montauban region in June 1944. A month earlier, General Lammerding had been named commander of the division, which was attached to General Kruger's 50th Armored Corps.

On June 5 Lammerding wrote Kruger about the measures to be taken against the "terrorists":[1]

The change in the situation of the maquisards in the Cahors-Aurillac-Tulle zone represents a danger which, in the event of a landing, might influence the course of the operations.

Most of the terrorists are pursuing destructive Communist objectives. And the population helps them only when forced to

---

1. Document quoted by Pierre-Yves Kervez in *Historama*.

do so (especially the wealthy and the functionaries). So far the measures taken against the terrorists have achieved little success. . . .

. . . The division regards the following measures as indispensable and also as the only ones likely to prove successful:

1) A powerfully launched counterpropaganda identifying the terrorists as troublemakers so that the civilian population will turn against them. . . .

2) The occupation of three towns—Cahors, Figeac, and Brive—by mobile units that will participate actively in the struggle against these bands and enlist in so doing the cooperation of the S.D. [*Sicherheitsdienst*]. . . . For more ambitious operations, a tank platoon and a motorized or armored battalion must be held in reserve. The 2nd S.S. Panzer division will have sole command of all units involved.

3) On June 15, 5,000 suspects are to be rounded up in the Cahors-Aurillac-Brive zone. They will be sent to Germany. According to information gleaned from the civilian population, the terrorists have been enrolling in this region the classes of 1945 and 1946. If these 5,000 men are subtracted, the terrorist organization will no longer have enough strength to launch any big operations.

4) On June 15, at least 200 trucks and 400 tourist buses will be rounded up in the Cahors-Aurillac-Brive region. In the event of a landing, the terrorists and the airlifted enemy will try to seize all available vehicles. . . . If we requisition all vehicles that are not absolutely indispensable to the economy, the enemy will lose an important part of his power.

5) In exchange for information about arms deposits, Maquis leaders, and so on, an imprisoned friend or family member will be released.

6) Let it be known that for every German wounded three terrorists will be hanged (not shot), and for every German killed ten terrorists will be hanged; then carry out this warning. . . .

The division is convinced that if these measures are carried out, the territory will be sufficiently pacified by June 15 so that, in the event of a landing, there will be no disturbances that might affect our operations. The forces involved are substantially smaller than those we would have to employ for big operations or for around-the-clock patrols. It is therefore absolutely necessary that we implement all the measures indicated with the requisite vigor.

General Kruger approved everything in Lammerding's plan. We shall see how rigorously these measures were enforced.

At this moment, the town of Tulle, in Corrèze, constituted a particularly sensitive spot. Along with a small German garrison belonging to the 95th security regiment, there was a 700-strong French "law and order" force comanded by Colonel Colomb.

Pierre Trouillé, the prefect of Corrèze, was an unusual personality who had close contacts with the Resistance. The prefect found himself in a most delicate situation. He knew that very serious events were in the offing. And he understood the German troops' state of mind as well as that of the forces of "law and order." His main concern was to protect the population.[2]

On June 6, Pierre Laval telephoned him from Vichy, and the two had the following exchange:

"Well, Trouillé, what's new since the day before yesterday?"

"The net is tightening, Monsieur le Président. The maquisards have begun to harass the law-and-order troops. We're expecting a general attack any minute."

"I can see that the situation is serious, Trouillé. I know that you're a brave man. You proved it at Saint-Malo and at Brest. You'll prove it again at Tulle. My greetings. Good luck. Goodbye, Trouillé."

"Monsieur le Président, I promise you that I'll do my duty as a prefect and a Frenchman."

And the prefect noted: "After this ironic remark, the conversation ended. As far as Vichy was concerned, I was already dead and buried."

---

2. Based on Pierre Trouillé's account in *Journal d'un Préfet pendant l'Occupation.*

During the night of June 6–7, the F.T.P. invaded Tulle. Around five in the morning, the first shots rang out over the barricades that had been erected at the end of the town. The attackers were armed with 20-millimeter cannon, mortars, rockets, and machine guns. The barricades, guarded by the *Gardes mobiles,* were quickly destroyed. Several days prior to the engagement, Resistance emissaries had tried to win over the *Gardes mobiles* and the G.M.R., apparently with some success, since they didn't put up much of a battle. The telephone call made by Colonel Colomb to the "law and order" command post at Limoges is revealing:

"If we keep on firing," he said, "the men on our side will join the Maquis."

The answer came: "If there's no other way out, retreat— that is, if you offer the Germans your protection."

Reichmann, the commander of the German garrison, in turn asked his superiors for directives. He was told to stay and fight.

The F.T.P. headquarters were moved to the town hall. By the end of the morning, the maquisards had contacted Colonel Colomb. They told him: "We have been charged by our comrades to ask the police, whom we have been forced by circumstances to attack, to surrender and join us. There is but one common enemy, and if we unite we'll be much stronger in opposing him."

Colomb asked the Prefect Trouillé to come and arbitrate. He told the prefect, "They're demanding unconditional capitulation. My sense of military honor will not allow me to yield to their demands. But I want you to decide."

Trouillé spoke incisively to the maquisards: "Enough French blood has already been shed. Conclude an immediate armistice to last for a few hours. The colonel has been ordered by his superiors to return to Limoges. He should be allowed to do so together with those of his men who choose to follow him. The *Francs-Tireurs* should permit the column to proceed, keeping with them any men who volunteer."

Everyone accepted this solution. A few *Gardes* joined the Maquis. Most of the Vichy forces finally left Tulle around four in the afternoon. But in the meantime the Germans had counterattacked, recapturing the railway station, where they shot eighteen railroad guards who had hidden in a coal bin. These men were neither maquisards nor fighters. Just one survived because he had the presence of mind to play dead after he was wounded.

The Germans finally withdrew to two strong points: a girls' school near the offices of the prefecture in the northern part of the town, and a munitions factory and the Souillac school in the southern section.

The fighting went on and on. The F.T.P. concentrated on the girls' school but with little success. Trouillé made the following notation on June 8:

> Around 4:00 P.M. a large F.T.P. contingent cut off the park near the terrace. I went out quickly and hailed the leader. He came up, saluted properly, and introduced himself. He was a young teacher, the commander of his company. . . . I accompanied him for a few yards into the park, then witnessed an extraordinary spectacle: Members of the F.T.P. were walking stiffly behind a balustrade which the Germans were riddling with bullets. Some fell, the rest kept on going. Weren't they willing to hide? They were not, the leader said; they placed all their pride in their unwillingness to take cover. What nerve, what style! And also what a lack of military training!

The situation was soon to take a dramatic turn. Colonel Monteil, in charge of the emergency Red Cross teams, made an appeal for help to Canon Mangematin, head of the local seminary:[3] "We must retrieve the bodies of nine German soldiers who were shot by the Maquis against the cemetery wall," he told the canon.

The canon learned from a maquisard what had happened: "The Germans emerged carrying a white flag. We let them come,

---

3. Based on the account of Georges Beau and Léopold Gaubusseau in *R-5*.

thinking they wished to surrender. But when they reached the middle of the road they began tossing grenades at us. And so we fired on the lot of them."

Dead German soldiers filled the streets of the Trech neighborhood. Blood flowed into the gutters. Canon Mangematin told the inhabitants that the sidewalks must be cleaned immediately. He was afraid that German reinforcements were on the way and that there would be reprisals. On Boulevard de Bournazel a truck driven by a member of the F.T.P. made a wrong turn and ran over a few bodies, leaving needless but terrible evidence of mutilation.

The Secret Army's leaders had tried to make the F.T.P. understand the dangers of attacking Tulle, and their fears, with those of the prefect and the canon, proved entirely justified. The "Das Reich" division was ordered, during the night of June 7–8, to go into action in the Tulle-Limoges sector. It was to "head toward Tulle to free encircled German units there."

During the evening of June 8, a youthful member of the F.T.P. went to see the Prefect Trouillé and introduced himself:

"My name is Kléber. I'm the commandant at Tulle."[4]

"What can I do for you?" the prefect asked.

Kléber replied, "You know, I am sure, that we, the Communist F.T.P., are the ones who conquered Tulle. We had an army of about 1,800 men, but with a mere seventy we managed to harass the so-called law-and-order forces. The Germans gave us more trouble, but we beat them. Now we still have a pocket in Souillac to clean out. Tomorrow it will be gone. I'm a soldier. I left my farm to fight, and I'm not finished yet. I have no interest in administration, but the running of this town must continue without interruption. We have proven by our attitude that we like and respect you. I suggest that you retain control of the administration under the supervision of a civic committee. In a few days, the Communist Party will make more complete arrangements."

---

4. This account is by Prefect Trouillé.

But the prefect had other ideas: "I can't accept your supervision. Either you trust me and I'll stay, or else you can go ahead and establish a supervisory group and I will retire to my chambers, where I will consider myself your prisoner."

"If that's the way you feel," Kléber retorted, "you'll have to take care of the administration yourself."

Trouillé mentioned the possibility that the Germans might return.

The F.T.P. commandant laughed. "Don't worry, you'll never see a Boche in Corrèze again."

Less than two hours later, the armored cars of the "Das Reich" division entered Tulle. The F.T.P.'s guerrilla forces immediately withdrew. Now the civilian population was left face to face with tragedy.

By the morning of June 9, the S.S. were everywhere, including the offices of the prefecture. The Germans discovered there a packing case filled with grenades, rifles, and automatic pistols which the law-and-order forces had left behind. Trouillé had planned to hand them over to the Maquis, and how was he going to explain them now?

The officer turned to the prefect: "You're nothing but a terrorist."

Trouillé recalled:

I received a beating with the butt of a Mauser pistol that came down hard on my kidneys and legs. Then I was dragged unceremoniously toward a hill close to the passage that led into my building. The S.S. deposited the incriminating evidence at my feet.

Still stunned by the blows, I saw eight soldiers step away from the others, form a line on the other side of the passage, come to attention a few yards from me. The officer passed on their right, then barked a sharp order. The S.S. loaded and raised their guns.

Realizing the fate that appeared to be in store for him, the prefect, striking his chest, shouted at the officer in German. The officer hesitated. Finding an S.S. man who spoke French, the prefect finally persuaded the officer to fetch his superior, and his life was spared.

The Germans meanwhile had begun to round up all the town's males, about 5,000 men and boys. They formed endless lines, shoved around by the S.S. Seeing the prefect in his uniform, they called to him, "Help us!"

"Take heart. We're about to plead your case," Trouillé answered. He noted:

> Such frightened crowds were to be seen everywhere. And the destruction! Telephone wires pulled up, windows broken, houses riddled with bullets. Pools of blood stained the sidewalks. Here and there lay the bodies of civilians. One of them sprawled on his back outside the Roubenne haberdashery store, his enormous belly swollen like a drowned man's.

The Germans set up their headquarters at the intersection of the Virevialle and Brive highways. After being kept waiting for a moment, the prefect was taken to a room where an officer, "cold but correct," introduced himself:

"Major Kowatch, the general's chief of staff."[5]

Trouillé pleaded with the man for a long time. The burden of his argument was that there was no connection between the inhabitants of Tulle and the Maquis. The terrorists had suddenly emerged from the woods and, after delivering their blow, had returned to the woods. Those who were really responsible for all this were far away.

The officer agreed to this and promised: "After making a careful check, I will authorize the release of all those who are 'indispensable.' "

The prefect said this would suffice. He would somehow

---

5. Actually, Stücker was the chief of staff. Kowatch was a subordinate staff officer.

manage to stretch to the utmost the meaning of the word "indispensable."

On orders from Kowatch, Trouillé returned to his office. In the course of the morning, the bishop, Monsignor Chassagne, the bursar, Lafue, and the mayor, Colonel Bouty, visited him with a proposal. Trouillé relates:

> All three expressed their distrust of the Germans' promise and declared with moving simplicity that they were prepared to offer themselves as hostages if that should be necessary in order to guarantee the good behavior of the population.

Shortly after 4:00 P.M. Kowatch came to deliver a message from the German command: "Because of your humane treatment of some of our wounded, the German High Command will cancel the order to burn down Tulle and shoot the entire male population. But the insult to the German flag cannot go unpunished. Therefore, 120 accomplices of the Maquis in Tulle —in other words, twice the number of comrades we found assassinated yesterday—will be hanged and their corpses thrown into the river."

"That's unjust!" the prefect exclaimed. "You know very well that the culprits are not in Tulle. You are about to kill innocent people. If you need hostages, take us, me first of all, and take the bishop too, and the bursar. Besides, that would prove more effective."

Kowatch looked at his watch. "Your gesture is grandiose but perfectly useless. The executions started five minutes ago."

How were the victims selected? Pierre Torquebiau tells us:[6]

> It was six o'clock in the morning when the S.S. man came to get me. "Don't be afraid," he said in excellent French, "you won't be the only one." And he was right. At the munitions factory where he took me, 5,000 men had already been assembled. After

---

6. Quoted in *Le Patriote résistant* of June 1969.

a check of their identities and occupations, only about 600 were detained. S.S. Officer Walter, the officer in charge, stalked around them like a hunting dog sniffing its quarry. Meanwhile, preparations had been made for the execution: ropes with slip-knots were attached to trees on the Rue des Martyrs [at that time, Rue Pont-Neuf], the balconies and lampposts, from the vicinity of the railroad station to the Virevialle highway—a distance of several hundred yards. Next to each knotted rope was a short stepladder flanked by two S.S. men who appeared to be delighted by the treat they were about to enjoy.

The doomed men were quickly brought to the execution site in groups of ten. Strangely enough, my group numbered thirteen. But they wanted ten, no more and no less. Thereupon Walter summoned Abbé Espinasse, the lycée's chaplain, who was there because he too had been arrested. At the moment he was offering spiritual solace to his companions. Walter asked him to select three men to be subtracted from my group, thus leaving only ten for the executioners.

The abbé refused to accept such an inhuman task, and the S.S. man made the selection. His eyes happening to fall on me, he asked me to step aside.

Abbé Espinasse, for his part, has written:[7]

As one can readily imagine, I refused to make a choice so cruel for a Frenchman, and I walked away to allow Lieutenant Walter to do as he pleased.

From a distance, I witnessed a touching scene. One of the soldiers in the firing squad allowed himself to be persuaded by the arguments of an intended victim. Taking the man by the arm, he walked over to his lieutenant and asked him to be merciful. The lieutenant agreed, and the man was saved! Then the young Frenchman and the very young armed and helmeted S.S., who was about to escort the remaining prisoners to the gallows, fell into each other's arms. I went up to the lieutenant, who said, not

---

7. Quoted in *R-5*.

without some emotion: "What that soldier did should not surprise you; he's an Alsatian."

Meanwhile, the rest of the scenario was proceeding as planned. Colonel Bouty described it to the prefect:

In front of the assembled captives, the men selected by the S.S. were taken off in groups of ten for execution. Abbé Espinasse offered them farewell words of solace. Almost all of them knelt as the abbé made the sign of the cross over their heads and gave them absolution. The group was quickly shoved toward the ropes which hung from balconies at the intersection of the Rue 4-Septembre and Rue Pont-Neuf. A plasterer's double stepladder of white wood was set up next to the gallows. The unfortunate men had to climb it. An S.S. officer mounted the steps of another ladder placed alongside the first and tied a rope around each victim's neck. Below, another S.S. man suddenly jerked away the ladder, leaving the victim dangling in the void. Occasionally, in order to speed up the hanging, the barbarians prodded the victim with the butts of their pistols and then, uttering savage cries, kicked aside the ladder, which fell. Meanwhile, with the volume raised to a maximum, loudspeakers blared dance music that was accompanied by the wild singing of the Nazis and carried all the way to the residential area.

One of the doomed men, François Teillé, managed to break loose, knock down his two guards, and dive headfirst onto the rocks overlooking the river. The S.S. finished him off with their guns.

The number thus executed came to ninety-nine. The youngest, Jean Vieillfond, was not yet eighteen; the oldest, Henry Maury, had just turned forty-six.

In the end, the Germans gave up the idea of throwing the bodies into the river. They ordered that their victims be buried anonymously and without delay in the household garbage dump at Cueille. The prefect, however, managed to be present at the burial, and Abbé Espinasse gave them all absolution. In addition, 149 were deported; of these, 101 were never to return to Tulle.

At the time of these terrible events in Tulle, other elements of the "Das Reich" division were doing their bloody work. Learning that the village of Argenton-sur-Creuse was in the hands of the F.F.I., General Lammerding had ordered the 15th company of the "Der Führer" regiment to retake it. As soon as the S.S. arrived, the maquisards left. Fifty-three inhabitants were killed. Sixteen hostages were selected by Captain Haelke, commander of the 15th company, and executed on the way back to the post.

That same day, June 9, a German truck proceeding from Limoges to Poitiers was captured by the Maquis. In the vehicle, besides the driver, was Obersturmführer Gerlach, an ordnance officer in the assault section of the "Das Reich" division who had been making arrangements to billet troops in the Nieul region.

Both men were stripped, beaten, and made to understand that they did not have long to live. Gerlach managed with great difficulty to make it clear that he was the ordnance officer of his division and that if he were taken to the head of the Maquis, he would provide important intelligence. Transported to Oradour-sur-Glane, he was not kept there long.

Gerlach has furnished the following account:[8]

[The truck] returned after two or three hours. Once again we were tied up before entering the vehicle. Then we were taken to a road in the woods. . . . The truck started down the road but after about 350 yards stopped alongside another French truck, easily recognizable because of its tricolor emblem. We were shoved from the vehicle very roughly, manhandled, and then dragged to a very young maquisard who seemed to be in charge. . . . Not bothering to interrogate us, he shouted: "I won't listen to the S.S. Put them to death immediately."

8. Quoted in *R-5*.

The two men were dragged into the forest. With all the fury of a desperate man, the driver put up a fierce battle, thereby monopolizing the attention of the other maquisards. Gerlach took advantage of the situation to escape and managed to reach his command post in Limoges the next morning, June 10.

Gerlach recounted his adventures to Colonel Stadler. A few hours later, Dickmann, commander of the 1st battalion of the "Der Führer" regiment, set out for Oradour-sur-Glane with orders to retaliate by taking and executing a large number of prisoners. A new and singularly horrifying tragedy was about to unfold.

June 10, a Saturday, was a bustling day in Oradour. People from Limoges, who had come to spend the weekend, took advantage of their visit to search for food. For smokers, it was the date for the second ten-day distribution of tobacco rations. And it was also the day that school children visited Doctor Desorteaux, the mayor, for their periodic physical checkup.

At 2:15 the Germans arrived. Monsieur Joyeux has provided the following account:[9]

> A few vehicles came and parked in the surrounding country-side. . . . Soldiers armed with automatic rifles and pistols got out and encircled the locality, shoving everyone encountered on roads and in farms toward the village square. Darting about in the fields, the S.S. hid in bushes to catch anyone who tried to escape. The farmers had to leave their work. Firing broke out. Several people were shot.

The Germans searched the village. Jean Darthout noted: "The S.S. entered all the houses in Oradour, opened every door and, threatening to kill, forced everyone, even people who were ill, to go to the village square."

Almost simultaneously, the schools were invaded by the Germans. They assembled all the children and told them to get

---

9. *Oradour-sur-Glane,* documents published by Office français d'Edition.

ready to leave. One hundred and ninety-one children were accompanied by two male and five female teachers.

The situation that prevailed by 2:45 P.M. has been described by Darthout:

> All the inhabitants of Oradour were soon rounded up in the main square of the village. Some women were in tears, others showed more courage or confidence. Some carried babies in their arms or pushed them in little carriages. I saw one woman supporting an old man who apparently had been forced to leave his bed. As for the men, some of them had been interrupted in the midst of their labors—the baker, his torso quite naked, was covered with flour.

At 3:00 P.M. the population was divided into two groups: on one side, the women and children; on the other, the men. The first group, surrounded by eight or ten members of the S.S., was taken to the church. The men were ordered to turn about and face the wall. Darthout ventured a quick backward glance.

> I saw a group of our mothers and helpmates who went off looking very sad. Some cried, others fainted. They had their arms around one another. I glimpsed my wife for the last time as she disappeared with the others at a turn in the street.

An interpreter appeared and said to the men: "There are clandestine depots here of arms and munitions collected by the terrorists. We are going to make a search. Meanwhile, to facilitate our work, we're going to put you in barns. If you know where any of these depots are, we urge you to tell us."

No one uttered a word. And for good reason: there were no arms depots in Oradour.

The men were divided up and moved into a number of barns. Monsieur Roby has recounted what happened next:

Four soldiers stood at the door, pointing their automatic rifles at us to prevent us from escaping. They talked among themselves and laughed as they examined their weapons. Suddenly, five minutes after we'd entered the barn, apparently obeying a signal—an explosion that seemed to come from some point in the village square—they uttered loud shouts and, like cowards, opened fire on us.

The men fell on top of one another. The wounded screamed. The S.S. officers approached the victims and shot on the spot any of the wounded who seemed to be stirring. They covered the bodies with straw, hay, and kindling wood, set them on fire, then left.

Roby was wounded in the elbow. Noticing a hole in the wall, he took refuge in a neighboring granary, where he discovered four of his friends. The five men managed to escape from the holocaust and sought refuge in the countryside.

In the church at Oradour where the women were confined, only one escaped: Madame Marguerite Rouffanche.[10] She has recounted the following ghastly story:

Around 4:00 P.M. twenty-year-old soldiers placed a kind of voluminous packing case in the nave near the altar from which hung strings that dragged on the floor.

Soon after these strings were set on fire, the flames reached the mechanism in the packing case, and a loud explosion occurred. A thick, black, suffocating smoke began to fill the air. Half asphyxiated and screaming with terror, women and children rushed to those parts of the church where one could still breathe. The door of the sacristy gave way, yielding to the irresistible weight of the terrified group. I too entered the sacristy, and resigning myself to my fate, sat down on a step of the stairs. My

---

10. That day, Madame Rouffanche lost her husband, her son, her two daughters and her seven-month-old grandson.

daughter joined me. Noting that the room was filled with people, the Germans subjected everyone who had sought refuge there to a savage beating. My daughter, who sat next to me, was killed by a bullet fired from somewhere outside. I owe my life to the fact that I shut my eyes and pretended to be dead.

There was a burst of gunfire in the church. Then straw, kindling wood, and chairs were thrown pell-mell over the bodies that lay on the flagstones.

Having escaped the slaughter without even a scratch, I took advantage of the cloud of smoke to slip behind the high altar.

There were three windows in this part of the church. Eyeing the largest, the middle one, I climbed the stepladder used to light the candles and tried to reach this window. I don't really know how I did it, but I had the strength of ten and managed to hoist myself to the window. The stained glass was broken and I flung myself at the opening that beckoned me. The jump down was over thirty-six feet! Then I fled to the church garden.

Raising my eyes, I saw that I had been followed up the ladder by a woman clutching a baby that she held out toward me from the top of the window. Then she jumped, falling beside me. Alerted by the baby's cries, the Germans machine-gunned us. My companion and her infant were killed. I myself was wounded as I ran toward an adjacent garden. Hidden behind rows of green peas, I waited with anguish for someone to come to my aid. I was rescued the following day at 5:00 P.M.

This horrible massacre took a toll of 634, but only fifty-one of the bodies could be identified.

The next day, Sturmführer Dickmann dispatched the following laconic report:

The S.S.P. Gr.-54 "D.F." continued their cleanup operations in the U sector on June 10 and 11, 1944.

On June 10 at 1:30 P.M. the 1st S.S. "D.F." encircled Oradour. After a search, the village was burned. Munitions were found in almost every house.

On June 11, two companies marched on Nieul-le-Château. The terrorists had evacuated the locality during the night.

Results: 548 enemy dead, one of our men wounded.

The affair created quite a stir among the Germans. As soon as he returned to Limoges, Dickmann reported to Colonel Stadler. He tried to soft-pedal his story, mentioning the supposed discovery of arms and munitions. As for the church, he explained, the women and children had been locked up in it "for their own protection." When the village was set on fire, he said, the flames reached the church, where the Maquis had placed explosives. The extreme heat had set them off.

Some of the soldiers talked, and when Stadler learned the truth, he flew into a rage at Dickmann. He sent a report to Lammerding demanding that Dickmann be court-martialed, which Lammerding approved. But Dickmann was never tried. He was killed in combat on the Normandy front.

CHAPTER TWELVE

CITADEL IN
THE VERCORS

IN THE ALPS southwest of Grenoble, the Vercors mountains, twenty-eight miles long and thirteen miles wide, are surrounded by dizzying approaches. At the time when they became a great Maquis stronghold, only eight roads led to the interior, and three of them traversed mountain ridges. Though isolated, the mountains commanded important lines of communication—highways and railways.

Pierre Dalloz, a member of Jean Giradoux's staff when Giradoux was commissioner-general for information in 1939–40, had taken refuge at a place along the coast of Sassenage, opposite the bluffs of Vercors. Dalloz studied maps of the mountains and, early in 1943, came up with an appraisal of their strategic possibilities:[1]

1. Quoted by Paul Dreyfus in *Vercors: Citadelle de Liberté*.

A kind of island of terra firma is to be found out there . . . protected on all sides by a wall of China. Access to the island is by way of a very few openings carved out of the rock. One could barricade them, stage surprise attacks, and launch battalions of parachutists. . . . The military value of such a region is striking. It would take only ten or so demolitions, easy to carry out and defend, to bar access to all armored cars.

After a few feelers had been extended, Dalloz met with General Delestraint at Bourg on February 10 to discuss the idea. With maps before them, Delestraint and Dalloz, with General Desmaze and Resistance leader Yves Farge, went into the matter carefully. From then on it was known as the "Montagnards" project.

A fortnight later, the go-ahead signal was given over the BBC: "The mountaineers must continue to climb to the top."

Dalloz then recruited his team: Remy Bayle de Jessé, Inspector of Waters and Forests for the northern section of the Vercors; Commander Marcel Pourchier, formerly director of the High Mountain Climbing School in Chamonix; Captain Alain Le Ray (son-in-law of François Mauriac and today a general), a young officer who commanded an artillery company at Ourcq in 1940 and had subsequently escaped from the Germans.

It was Le Ray, together with Dalloz, who was to finalize the plan for putting the Vercors to military use. The plan called for a force of 7,500 men under fifteen commands, plus 450 scouts. The weapons were to include 795 machine guns, 795 automatic rifles, 6,360 pistols and carbines, five anti-tank cannon, and fifteen mortars. The ammunition was to amount to ten times the weight of these weapons.

According to Dalloz,

it was not merely a question of confronting a fully armed enemy, but rather of throwing him into greater disorder by attacking.

Nor was it a matter of digging in in the Vercors. Rather, we were to install ourselves there by stealth with the object of sallying forth to attack. This would not be a holding operation; instead, we were to push forward in every direction. The static exterior should not deceive us. Far from being frozen, the positions taken up could suddenly flame into explosive action.

On March 24, shortly after returning to France from London, General Delestraint himself came to inspect the Vercors.

Ever since the preceding December, a Maquis group connected with the *Francs-Tireurs* had been staying at the Ambel farm in the Vercors. By February 1943 eighty-five men had gathered there. As the number of volunteers increased, a system of surveillance and screening was established, and Eugène Chavant was put in charge of interrogating new recruits. The number of camps increased markedly. Seven new ones were established between February and May, 1943.

On May 27, 1943, an operation against an enemy tank-car failed, with disastrous consequences. Fourteen maquisards from the plateau were caught by the Italian Bolzano battalion, and the O.V.R.A. (*Opera Vigilanza Repressione Antifascista*) immediately took over. The captives gave a confused account in response to questioning, and several people with Resistance ties, including Yves Farge's wife and son, were placed under arrest.

Farge was forced to leave the region. Before doing so, he briefed Captain Le Ray and turned over to him his modest war treasury. Dalloz refrained from returning to his home and hurriedly warned Delestraint that it would be dangerous to go back to Grenoble at that moment. A few days later—in his last message prior to his arrest in Paris on June 9—the general told Le Ray, "I authorize you to continue preparations for the execution of our initial plan. But I advise you to make sure that the organization incurs as few risks as possible."

For the men of the Vercors, the work that had to be done

now involved total reorganization. Eugène Chavant, who was obliged to disappear for a while, cautiously renewed his contacts and, at the urging of his comrades, became the civilian head of the Vercors.

The problem at this point was one of uniting the Vercors fighters. Since the mountains span two departments, the area was divided into two sectors: the north, commanded by Costa de Beauregard (Durieux), and the south, directed by Geyer (Thivollet). A second military committee for all the Vercors was established which included Chavant, Jean Prévost, Dr. Ravalec, Le Ray, and Costa de Beauregard.

Le Ray noted:[2] "For the immediate present, we could count on nine undermanned camps that were static in nature, and also on five 'sedentary' and rather embryonic companies formed in the canton of Villard-de-Lans and its environs."

On August 10, 1943, the civilian and military leaders of the Vercors met in Arbounouse. The five members of the military committee drafted a lengthy statement of how they planned to proceed.

The Arbounouse plateau was the scene of the first parachute drop on November 13. About a hundred containers filled with weapons, explosives, ammunition, pharmaceutical products, blankets, and clothing were brought in. But part of the shipment was picked up by local teams that paid little heed to the plan for distributing the drop, with unfortunate repercussions.

Reproached about the conditions under which the parachuted equipment had been received, Le Ray resigned. This news so greatly affected the leaders of the Vercors that Chavant decided to announce the dissolution of the local Maquis. It was Le Ray himself who induced him to reverse his decision.

Captain Geyer was named head of the Vercors Maquis. He did not enjoy the wholehearted confidence of Chavant and his

---

2. Quoted by Paul Dreyfus.

associates. Since Dalloz had gone to Algiers and Le Ray had been relieved of his duties, the Vercors no longer had anyone who was familiar with the original objectives of the "Montagnard" plan.

While these changes were being made—and they inevitably affected the conduct of future operations—the situation in the area occasionally caused a good deal of anxiety.

Delestraint had hoped that the Vercors maquisards would refrain from taking any unnecessary risks until the appointed time, when Allied operations would be concentrated on the western front. But it was not easy to hold back young people eager to do battle against the invaders.

Thus, on January 18, 1944, at the Goule Noire bridge, a group of maquisards captured two German civilians and a man who claimed to be a Dutch journalist. Two days later, a detachment of the Feldgendarmerie came up to the Vercors to investigate. Their car was intercepted on the Rousset hill by a *groupe-franc*. The driver was killed and another occupant of the vehicle wounded. But two Germans who managed to escape sounded the alarm.

On January 22 a German column traversed the Vercors from Sainte-Eulalie to La Chapelle-en-Vercors. The column comprised a light armored car, two 37-millimeter cannon, thirty trucks, and a few motorcycles—300 men in all. Several times they scuffled with groups of maquisards who, in spite of frenzied efforts, were unable to stop them.

This was evidence that the Germans could penetrate the base at will. Instead of profiting by the experience, the maquisards made plans to reinforce the plateau's defenses.

On January 29 a group independent of the Vercors organization, the Maquis of Malleval, were attacked by the enemy. Numbering about fifty men, they were commanded by Lieutenant Gustave Eysseric, a former officer of the 6th B.C.A. (Alpine *Chasseurs*). Their camp was surrounded. Eysseric was killed in the fighting, as were thirty other men. Eight civilians or maquisards were burned alive in a farmhouse. The presbytery which had served as the command post was dynamited.

After this terrible experience, it was decided that the nucleus of the 6th B.C.A. would have to be transferred to the center of the Vercors, where things were better organized. In anticipation of the landings, a regional command post was set up at a place called La Matrassière, near Saint-Julien. But the Germans undoubtedly were well informed. On March 18 they launched a surprise attack against the post and succeeded in taking it. Several officers and men were killed.

The Vercors was now isolated in the face of the enemy. Several farmhouses were burned down in Saint-Julien. In the Borel farmhouse, Germans discovered an abandoned weapon. They forced Monsieur Borel, an elderly peasant, to march around the building several times carrying a heavy burden. Whenever the old man stopped, exhausted, they beat him, in front of his wife and his son. Meanwhile, the farmhouse was burning. A young maquisard who had sought refuge in the granary was charred to death beneath bundles of straw.

Early in April, a force of 500 security policemen took up quarters in La Chapelle-en-Vercors and Vassieux. Houses were searched and checkups instituted. The "law-and-order" men proceeded to interrogate, torture, and carry out summary executions. They set fires, pillaged, and handed young men over to the Germans for deportation.

The main objective of the Maquis at this time was to obtain more outside help in equipping the Vercors. An Englishman, H. Thackwaite, who headed the so-called "Union" mission, was parachuted to the Vercors. Upon his return to London on May 3, he handed in a report requesting the dispatch of heavy machine guns and mortars. But he was accorded a cool reception. "There are scarcely enough mortars for the regular army," he was told.

Eugène Chavant, for his part, went to Algiers in the latter

part of May and called on officers of de Gaulle's Special Projects Operations Center. They promised to airlift 4,000 men to the Vercors. Chavant returned the day after the Normandy landings with a paper in his pocket dated May 30 and signed by Jacques Soustelle, in the name of General de Gaulle. It read:

The directives issued in February 1943 by General V [Vidal —Delestraint's code name] for the organization of the Vercors remain valid.

They will be implemented under the supervision of the D.M.R.I. [local Gaullist Resistance leaders] in liaison with both the Maquis mission sent from London and the commander of the base in Algiers.

A number of changes in command were made. Captain Le Ray was named departmental head of the F.F.I., succeeding Reyniès, who had just been arrested by the Gestapo following a denunciation by a Frenchman.[3] Squadron leader François Huet was appointed head of the entire Vercors Resistance.

June 6 signaled the start of real mobilization. One witness, Roland Bechmann-Lescot, has recalled it:

From all around—Grenoble, Romans, and other places, by all and every means of locomotion—on foot, by car and bus; in innumerable vehicles that would prove invaluable for external liaison, some of which had been pinched from their owners, the volunteers summoned by the Vercors leaders came together, to the great annoyance of the Germans. They joined forces with an eagerness that was reminiscent of the 1793 conscription. Assembled in previously prepared mobilization centers, they received a medical checkup and were then organized and equipped.

On June 8 Colonel Descour, F.F.I. regional commander, came to the Vercors and set up headquarters in a house in the

---

3. He was tortured by the Gestapo, and his body has never been recovered.

forest of Rang-des-Purrets, near Saint-Agnan. Five civilian camps were organized: the Belmont company (Captain Paul Brisac), comprising people from Grenoble, was stationed at Saint-Nizier; the Fayard company (Captain Bordeaux), recruited in Royans, occupied the forest of Lente; the Philippe company (Captain Henri Ulmann) prepared to defend the Coulmes forest; the Abel company (Captain Crouau), composed of men from Romanais, assembled in Balme de Rencurel; the Goderville company (Captain Jean Prévost), made up of former *groupes-francs* from the plateau's communes, moved toward Saint-Nizier to join the Belmont company.

Commander Pierre Tanant, who furnished the above details, has summed up:

> Within a few days our forces had increased from 500 to almost 3,000. Volunteers continued to flow toward us uninterruptedly until July 20; on the day of the big battle, between 4,000 and 5,000 fighters were in the besieged fortress.
>
> Between Saint-Nizier and Vassieux in an area that included Coulmes, the Goule Noire, the Goulets, and the Rousset hills, all the roads were sealed and the approaches carefully watched. Command posts were set up and a provisioning service functioned. A general feeling of good will prevailed. The inhabitants made common cause with their defenders.
>
> The weather was magnificent in that month of June. The sky was a dazzling blue; at a height of 2,800 feet, the air was delightful. But mainly one felt free up there on the green mountain tops.

Amid this euphoria—which was not necessarily shared either by Chavant or by Huet—a telegram from London received on June 10 caused not a little surprise. The message in effect ordered demobilization, in keeping with a decision that General Koenig had just relayed to all Resistance organizations: "Slow down to the utmost all guerrilla activity. Impossible as of the moment to provide sufficient weapons and ammunition. Break off contact everywhere whenever possible in preparation for the reorganization phase. Avoid large gatherings. Organize small, isolated groups."

The commander-in-chief of the F.F.I. was more precise on June 16:

> The mission of any interior army is to fight. Almost all aviation is currently being used by the High Command for direct support of the bridgehead. The arming and equipping of the F.F.I. can only be accomplished gradually. Therefore we are forced to equip units on the basis of priority in zones now involved in the battle for the liberation of France. Until such time as plans for obtaining weapons and ammunition can be realized, avoid gathering unarmed units around forces already formed.

But it was too late to shift into reverse. Although the Allies sent messages to spur insurrection throughout France, they did so in order to avoid premature revelation of the principal landing zone of the Allied armies, and also to spread doubt about the sites of subsequent operations. And indeed, no one, least of all the maquisards, could believe that the Provence landing would fail to take place before August 15. The French Resistance was to pay dearly in every region for this wartime strategy, but nowhere were the consequences more serious than in the Vercors.

As early as June 10, three messages were sent to Algiers. Descour dispatched the first appeal: "Vercors, 2,000 volunteers to be armed. Initial enthusiasm undermined by failure send promised arms. Extremely urgent. Need men, weapons, tobacco here within forty-eight hours maximum. Full-strength attack possible. Under present conditions, impossible to resist. Failure to comply will entail merciless reprisals. Would be disastrous for regional Resistance."

The next day he sent a follow-up message: "For Vercors, I repeat, urgent need for Maquis-type arms for eighteen light companies, heavy weapons for six companies. Once armed, these forces will prove absolutely indispensable to Vercors. They will then be ready for offensive operations in all directions. Mobilization has been ordered on strength of formal assurances we would receive weapons. Failure to keep promise immediately will create tragic situation. Best regards."

The situation did in fact deteriorate quickly, for the Germans were not long in reacting. On June 13 they attacked Saint-Nizier. Around 9:30 A.M. the first shots were fired at the advance posts near Guillets, a few miles from Grenoble.

The Germans had infiltrated the woods and thickets that bordered the Pariset road. The maquisards had a hard time containing the enemy. An infantry platoon commanded by the head adjutant, Chabal, arrived in an armored car, and this enabled the maquisards to launch a counterattack. Their losses were heavy, but the enemy, now in disarray, decided to go back to Grenoble. In fact, the intensity of the battle led the Germans to evacuate the posts they had set up in Seyssins and Seyssinet at the foot of the plateau.

Captain Tanant noted:

> The night is beautiful. The stars are shining. Algiers has just announced a parachute drop; the usual message has just been heard over the BBC. We are delighted because we urgently need arms and munitions to resist an imminent assault.
>
> At our feet is Grenoble, where a number of our men and their families are sleeping peacefully. Around two in the morning the familiar blare of the sirens can be heard.

Planes now arrived and dropped their cargoes. The containers were picked up quickly, and the weapons in them cleaned, reassembled, and distributed.

Greater optimism began to prevail, which Tanant expressed:

> The parachute drop tonight, arriving just in time, fills us with confidence and seems to reduce the distance between us and our North African friends. We are all involved in the same war. Since they certainly do not suffer from a lack of supplies, they will parachute in everything we need.

On June 15, at five in the morning, the Germans resumed their attack, but this time with more powerful weapons. The maquisards fought courageously, but positions were quickly reversed. The enemy infiltrated everywhere. By ten o'clock the order to retreat had to be given.

The Germans entered Saint-Nizier and burned it almost to the ground. The bodies of maquisards recently buried in the cemetery were dug up and thrown into the flames.

During those three days, the Vercors lost twenty-four men. But it inflicted far heavier losses on the Germans.

An anguished message was sent to Algiers: "We've been attacked in force. We urge you to hurry. You are putting us in a catastrophic position. We're run out of ammunition. You bear full responsibility for our resistance."

On June 20 the Germans attacked the plateau of Combovin, one of the Vercors's advance posts, destroying the F.F.I.'s transmission center and massacring six radio and telephone operators. This experience served to underscore the danger created for the Vercors by the proximity of the Chabeuil airfield. Colonel Descour asked the Allied aviation to bombard it, stressing the presence there of sixty enemy planes. Meanwhile, the maquisards succeeded in bringing down two Junker planes, using only their automatic weapons.

Profiting by a moment of respite, the Vercors organized its administrative and military services as it readied itself for the enemy's next attack. Captain Tanant noted:

> One of our first visitors was Yves Farge, named by Algiers as commissioner of the Republic in the Rhône-Alpes region. He spelled out the role of the civil and military authorities and gave precise instructions in order to effect as close a liaison as possible between the two. By his presence he consecrated the Free Republic of Vercors, symbol of the future of Free France.

Farge set up his "prefectural staff" at La Chapelle-en-Vercors. Sunday, June 25, was a great day for the maquisards, for out of a cloudless sky thirty-six flying fortresses dropped more than 800 containers over the Vessieux terrain during the course of the morning. It was the first daytime parachute drop.

Tanant has described it:

> It was a unique spectacle: hundreds of multicolored parachutes descending in compact clusters, disappearing behind the wooded mountain crests to land on meadows and fields. In this fashion, we received a quantity of weapons and ammunition that would enable us not only to finish equipping our own troops but also to come to the aid of neighboring Maquis groups. This massive parachute drop was in addition to more modest ones that had taken place during the preceding nights.

But even more important for the morale of the Vercors men was the arrival during the night of June 28–29 of two commando outfits dropped by plane on the Vassieux terrain. Each unit numbered fifteen men. The newcomers included Americans serving under Captain Tuppers as well as members of the "Eucalyptus" mission commanded by Major Desmond Longe.

This parachute drop was soon followed by another—the "Paquebot" mission, under Captain Tournissa. Tournissa was to set up an air field capable of receiving heavy weapons which could not be dropped in containers.

On July 10 Tuppers's men joined a platoon of the 11th company.[4] That same day, a bus took the men to the Menée pass, where they prepared an ambush along national highway 75, near the Lus-la-Croix-Haute pass. The maquisards withdrew after killing about forty Germans. The French suffered two casualties, the Americans none.

"The teams of Captain Tuppers and Major Longe," Tanant noted, "continued uninterruptedly to work with their Algerian or British opposite numbers, and we had the feeling of being backed up."

---

4. Twenty-four men from the Bourgeois squadron and fifteen Americans.

This impression was confirmed on July 11 by a message from General Koenig which stated:

> Free French Fighters of the Interior at Vercors: For three years you in the Vercors have been preparing for the struggle by leading a rough life in the Maquis.
>
> On D-day you took up arms and, offering heroic resistance to all enemy assaults, once again you flew the French flag and the emblem of Liberation over one corner of our French land.
>
> To you, F.F.I. fighters, and to the courageous inhabitants of the Vercors who have helped you, I address my congratulations and the vow that your successes will spread rapidly over our entire territory.

In all such official pronouncements there is some exaggeration, as, for example, the phrase "for three years."

During the morning of July 14, forty-eight American flying fortresses arriving from England dropped 860 containers over the terrain at Vassieux. This was part of a large-scale operation, christened "Cadillac," that embraced the Limousin and the Saône-et-Loire. This time the Germans reacted. Their planes had bombarded Vassieux and La Chapelle-en-Vercors the day before, causing casualties among both maquisards and civilians. Now, immediately after the parachute drop, enemy planes appeared above the Vercors. They carried on continuously until night fell, igniting houses or blowing them up.

That morning, Bastille day was celebrated at Saint-Martin-en-Vercors with a parade, flag displays, and music. All this occurred in the presence of the civil and military authorities. Yves Farge went to Die, where another parade was being held, complete with the bestowal of decorations. As he returned to the Vercors that evening, he noticed fires in the distance. This is what he found on his arrival at La Chapelle:

> Everything was in flames. We were in the midst of a conflagration. The heat was stifling. I found Chavant at the head of

a rescue team. The Beylier hotel was ablaze. . . . Toward the rear a man was seated all alone. He had stuck a candle in a bottle and was consuming a roast ham with extraordinary voracity. We had to swear at him to get him out; he consented to leave only after he had gathered up all the food his arms could hold.

The man was probably a Parisian who had lost his way.

The situation now began to deteriorate rapidly. Large concentrations of German troops belonging to General Pflaum's 157th division were spotted at Valence and at the Lus-la-Croix-Haute pass. On July 18 the enemy attacked the Grimone pass. Although reinforced, the maquisards were compelled to fall back after twenty-four hours of fighting.

On July 21 the Germans left Crest and headed for Die. They were ambushed and lost more than eighty men (thirty of whom were killed outright), plus a machine gun and several trucks. Nonetheless, they continued their advance. Another ambush at Espenel failed to prevent a large German column from advancing over the mountain tops. The Maquis had to withdraw.

Commanding officer Huet, who covered the Vercors untiringly, encouraging propitious offensives, correcting mistakes, and communicating his enthusiasm to everyone, nonetheless harbored few illusions. In the morning of July 22, he said to Tanant, "You see, my dear Laroche [Tanant's code name], we've embarked on a big, a very big venture. I have always believed that nine out of ten would never return. And yet we didn't have the right to say no."

Tanant noted, "Fortunately this remark proved to be overly pessimistic; more of us returned from this venture than he had anticipated."

Yves Farge, for his part, made a final request to the National Council of the Resistance in a letter of July 16:

Ever since June 6, we have accepted the risks of war even though we have no military role to perform. I believe—and I have said so—that we have had quite a bit of luck on our side and that it would be criminal to squander it by allowing each of the liberated regions to be attacked, especially in view of the fact that our base in Ardèche-Drône-Ain poses a real threat to all of the enemy's communications.

At 6:00 P.M. on July 21, a German column of 2,000 men, supported by artillery, left Saint-Nizier and headed for Villard-de-Lans. The drenching rain did not halt their progress. Around eight o'clock the 1st company of the 8th B.C.A. opened fire on them. At Jaume, the German column split into two groups. One marched toward Autrans through the Croix-Perrin pass; the other continued on the road to Villard-de-Lans.

Southeast of the Vercors, several small German columns left Trièves. Traversing Gresse, Saint-Michel-les-Portes and Chichilianne, they advanced toward Les Pas and the Grand-Veymont mountain peak. From there they would be able to penetrate the Vercors.

At 9:30 A.M. twenty aircraft appeared, flying close to the ground under a low ceiling. A glider was spotted. For a moment there was elation fueled by the hope that this was part of an Allied airlift. But in fact these were German planes, and they were making good use of the new Vassieux air strip which the "Paquebot" mission had built. This enemy operation, which had been minutely planned, took the Vercors completely by surprise. Ten gliders landed on the southern edge of Vassieux, three landed at Jossaulx, two at La Mure, two at the château, and two more at Chaux. In record time the attackers achieved their objectives, despite vigorous resistance from such men as young Jacques Descour, the colonel's son, who was killed firing his machine gun.

Aided by aerial reconnaissance, the Germans saw a chance to intervene faster than the Allies when they realized how perfectly the air strip had been readied: a field 3,300 feet long and 450 feet wide. The gliders landed 400 S.S. men led by Commander Schäfer. Only one glider crashed on landing.

The maquisards launched a counterattack against Vassieux,

but it failed. The S.S. had dug in solidly amid the ruins of the village. North of the Vercors, the Germans occupied the Croix-Perrin pass and entered Autrans about 5:00 P.M., in spite of attempts to counterattack.

Around noon they occupied Corrençon. There they clashed with the 4th company of the 6th B.C.A., whose fire was well aimed. But the company did not attempt to force a way through.

Roche-Pointue and the opening of the Bourne gorges toward Villard-de-Lans were held by the 3rd company of the 6th B.C.A. The road that was blocked by this force was strategically important, because it linked Villard to Méaudre through Jarrands. The 3rd company maintained contact with the 2nd, which held a key position at Valchevrière.

A decisive conference was held that evening at Huet's command post. Present were Colonel Henri Zeller, head of the F.F.I. in the southeast, Major Longe, Chavant, and several staff officers. They weighed three possible solutions:

1) To attempt a massive penetration of the enemy's lines. This, however, was not possible. Maquis units were engaged in combat over a 120-mile front. There was neither enough time nor the necessary means to round them up.

2) To attempt to pierce the lines in small groups. The losses were bound to prove enormous because the efforts would be so dispersed.

3) To keep fighting until all available means had been exhausted and then to fall back in small units, thereby creating a void in front of the enemy—in other words, to convert the Maquis into an out-and-out guerrilla force.

The last solution was unanimously adopted. Tanant remarked: "Alas! Many misunderstood it, and this was the cause of some of our losses. Only seasoned maquisards like those under Thivollet and Durieu executed it to the letter. The strategy was quite familiar to them, and they had always carried it out successfully."

The conferees also decided to evacuate the military hospital in the region of Die, where about forty men were being cared for. If the German advance should make such an evacuation impossible, the wounded were to be moved to the grotto of Luire. That night Captain Volume (Conus) left the Vercors. He was to contact Captain Le Ray as soon as possible and instruct him to attack the enemy's rear between Sassenage and the Grimone pass.[5]

With the approval of Huet, Chavant sent a stirring message to Algiers: "La Chapelle, Vassieux, Saint-Martin bombarded by German planes. Enemy troops parachuted to Vassieux. Demand immediate bombardment. Had promised to hold out for three weeks. Now six weeks since establishment of our organization. Request additional men, food, and matériel. Morale of the population excellent, but they will quickly turn against you if you do not take immediate steps, and we would have to agree with them that the leaders in Algiers and London do not understand the situation we find ourselves in and can be considered cowards and criminals. We mean what we say: cowards and criminals."

There is a second postdated version of this telegram, but the testimony of the protagonists themselves suggests that the above text is authentic.

Upon receipt of the telegram, Jacques Soustelle telephoned General Cochet, military delegate for the southern theater of operations. "You must send commandos to the Vercors immediately," he said.

But he failed to obtain them. Allied headquarters was concentrating all its attention on the landing in the Provence. At that time even the Italian campaign was considered to be of secondary importance. And so the fate of the Vercors was decided.

On the evening of July 22 another counterattack aimed at dislodging the Germans from Vassieux ended in failure. Earlier the same day, the Germans had seized Pas-des-Chattons and

---

5. Volume accomplished his mission but barely escaped being shot by the Germans.

Pas-de-la-Selle. This enabled them to install several mortars and
a few cannon which they then used to batter the plateau of
Grande Cabane. Little by little, they occupied the mountain
tops, precluding any effective counteraction by the Maquis.

Farther south, the Germans kept advancing toward Die. They
paid dearly for the seizure of Saillans, but on July 22 they occupied Die. At the hospital, all the wounded maquisards were massacred in the presence of horrified nuns.

The decisive phase of the struggle for the Vercors took place
in the Valchevrière sector on July 23. This area, commanded by
Jean Prévost (code name Goderville), extended to Collet de la
Coinchette, five miles south. The Goderville group comprised
the 2nd and 4th companies of the 6th B.C.A. The most sensitive
spot was north of the line, manned by Chabal's company.

Around 3:00 P.M. on July 22, the Germans sent out large
reconnaissance forces. In accordance with a prearranged plan,
the advance units fell back under the enemy's violent fire. Chabal
then counterattacked, righting the situation. But the night
brought no respite to the maquisards, who remained poised to
intercept endless German patrols.

In the morning, enemy mortars went into action, spraying
the Valchevrière-Herbouilly zone. At six o'clock advance units
infiltrated the pine forest. The men fell, one after the other:
Lieutenant Passy, infantrymen Jo Perrin and Mulheim.

Pierre Tanant has recalled the end of Valchevrière:

> Chabal remained as calm and self-controlled as if he were on
> maneuvers. Standing behind a rampart and taking careful aim,
> he fired his bazooka.[6]
>
> Pipe in his mouth, he never took his eyes off the Germans,
> as if challenging them by his sangfroid. His infantrymen watched
> him. This was certainly one of those moments in life when the
> importance of example was most evident.

---

6. He fired the bazooka twenty-seven times.

After an instant's hesitation, and in spite of their losses, the Germans continued their advance and managed to get a foothold on the rocky cliffs that dominated the Belvédère. At this point, Captain Goderville attempted a maneuver in an effort to get his lieutenant out of a tight spot.

But the enemy, clearly far stronger, could not be stopped.

As the ranks around Chabal thinned out, he sent the following message to Goderville: "I'm almost completely encircled. We are getting ready to execute a Sidi-Brahim.[7] Long live France!"

At eleven o'clock the battle was still raging, and as Tanant relates:

> Suddenly Lieutenant Chabal fell. Although gravely wounded, he got up and continued to fire. Then, remembering that he was carrying a small notebook in which the names of all his infantrymen were listed, he threw it over the parapet of the Belvédère to make sure that the Germans would not find it on his person. At this very same instant, he was wounded again, this time mortally, and sank to the ground.

The remaining members of the small group slowly retreated toward Herbouilly. Simultaneously, the Pas-de-la-Sambue defenses opposite Herbouilly were being forced. Concluding that the situation was hopeless, Goderville dispatched a last message to Huet. The game was up. Huet and his companions headed for the Lente forest, an almost inaccessible mountainous area southwest of the Vercors.

During the night of July 24–25, Huet sent Algiers a message in which he expressed in moderate but stern language the opinion of all Vercors fighters: "Vercors defenses pierced the 23rd at 4:00 P.M. after fifty-six hours of battle. Have ordered dispersal

---

7. At the shrine of Sidi-Brahim on September 26, 1845, the last squadron of the 8th infantry battalion of Orléans held out to the very end, executing a sortie which only one corporal and ten infantrymen survived.

in small groups in order to resume the fight if that should prove possible. Everyone has performed his duty courageously in a desperate struggle, but we are saddened at being obliged to yield because of the enemy's numbers and at having been completely abandoned while the battle was in progress."

In his memoirs, Jacques Soustelle discusses the question of whether it would have been possible to save the Vercors:

> To tell the truth, I don't think so; or rather, I think it would have required far greater means than those we could muster even in the best of circumstances. Against the Germans we would have had to pit forces of equal or comparable strength supported by heavy weapons and by numerous planes with a tremendous cruising capacity. Because they still controlled the territory, the Germans could concentrate men and matériel against a single objective whenever they chose to do so; therein lay their superiority.

While the maquisards of the Vercors were attempting to break out of the encirclement or retreating to the densest part of the forest, the Germans staged a series of reprisals. They massacred the inhabitants of Vassieux and executed the hostages they were holding in La Chapelle as well as all the maquisards they could get their hands on. A number of magnificent men, including Jean Prévost, talented writer and heroic fighter, thus disappeared.

Perhaps the worst atrocity perpetrated by the Germans was the massacre of the wounded at Die.

A letter found on a German prisoner described these gruesome happenings and, in a curiously boastful vein, even exaggerated them: "We have exterminated all the occupants of a hospital, including doctors and nurses. There were about forty of them. We dragged them out and shot them down with our automatic pistols. That may seem atrocious, but those dogs didn't deserve anything better."

Colonel Henri Zeller, military delegate for southeastern France, managed to leave the region on July 22, arriving in Algiers on August 3. Received by General de Gaulle, he explained the existing situation in the Alps, including the Vercors. "Thanks to their weapons—their cannon, mortars, tanks, and planes—the Germans are still capable of carrying out terrible reprisals. But once they have done so, they return to huddle in their garrisons. They do not dare to send an isolated car or a liaison agent out on the road. The railroad lines are blocked. One out of every two truck convoys transporting provisions is attacked, despite armed protection.

"The Germans, who will never dare to surrender to the 'terrorists,' are hoping almost as much as we are for the arrival of the Allied troops."

De Gaulle handed him a blue file. "The Allies will be landing on the coasts of the Provence in a few days," he said. "Here are the main features of the operations plan. Sit down at this table, study them, and give me your opinion."

Zeller scrutinized the document. He jumped up upon reading: "Grenoble, D-day plus 90." To himself he said: "The Allies won't reach Grenoble until three months after the landing! That's not possible. We'll all be dead by then."

He gave de Gaulle his opinion:

"This projected maneuver is overly timid. The mountain range is virtually in the hands of the F.F.I. Once the coastal area has been occupied to points twelve miles inland, the Allies must be audacious and not hesitate to send out light columns, supported by armored cars and cannon, on all the north-south roads."

Zeller indicated the itinerary to be followed, pointing out that the initial forces did not have to be large—1,500 to 2,000 men. With powerful assistance from the F.F.I., these columns would have an easy time capturing the German garrisons in Sisteron, Digne, Gap, etc.

De Gaulle decided to send Zeller to Naples to see General

Patch, commander of the American 7th Army, who was in charge of the landing operations, and General de Lattre, commander of France's B army. Zeller had his way, and events proved him right. The survivors of Vercors were to have many more opportunities to demonstrate their courage and fighting skill.

CHAPTER THIRTEEN

THE LIBERATION
OF PARIS

B Y THE SUMMER of 1944, the F.F.I. had about 20,000 troops in the department of the Seine. Their arms consisted only of about 1,800 rifles and 240 light machine guns. Colonel Rol-Tanguy, a Communist, directed operations in the Ile-de-France; Colonel Lizé (de MargueritTes), a de Gaulle loyalist, was in charge in the rest of the department.

The first mass demonstration against the enemy in Paris took place on Bastille day, July 14, in the eastern districts of the capital. It was organized by Toudic and Grodzinski, Communist members of a trade-union confederation, the *Union des Syndicats,* and supported by the F.T.P. The demonstrators controlled the streets for three-quarters of an hour. Arrested by the police, the two organizers tried to escape. Toudic was killed, and thus became the first casualty of the Paris insurrection.

On the morning of August 7, General von Choltitz was received by Hitler at his headquarters in the bunker of the Berlin chancellery. The Führer told him, "General, you are to leave for Paris. Maintain order in that city, which serves as a staging area for our troops. Stay in touch with Oberg. You will have my complete support. I am appointing you commander-in-chief of our troops. You will have as much absolute authority as a general can receive. You will wield powers like those exercised by the commander of a besieged fortress."

Von Choltitz noted:

> This visit [to the Führer's headquarters] destroyed the few illusions I might have retained. It was my personal conviction that the man who led us was hopelessly mad, that he was deceiving himself and everyone else.

Von Choltitz arrived in Paris on the evening of August 9. There he found that a good many higher-ups and their staffs were preparing to leave or had already left. Departing with them were troops attached to general headquarters, to the telecommunication services, and to numerous anti-aircraft batteries—approximately 6,000 in all.

On August 15 von Choltitz received an order to blow up the bridges of Paris. Some engineers were dispatched to carry out the mission. Von Choltitz noted:

> The more I thought about the planned demolitions, the more convinced I became of the line I would follow. I was supposed to maintain order and unity among my troops and make sure that the retreating forces would be able to traverse the city without difficulty. On the basis of my knowledge of the situation, I would have to decide whether such demolitions would serve my purposes. Actually, they would only make my task more difficult. Such purely military considerations aside, as a decent soldier I had already decided to do whatever I could to spare the population and the magnificent city of Paris. This resolve, rooted in my conception of the military profession, led me to attempt the impossible in order to save Paris from destruction.

Little by little, tension in the capital mounted. The BBC had announced on August 12 that certain Allied operations would no longer be reported. The Germans, now short of reconnaissance planes, would thus be kept in the dark. Between this deliberately curtailed flow of news and the tall tales aired over Radio-Paris, the Parisians were soon at the mercy of the wildest rumors. Yet life went on.

Jean Galtier-Boissière has described Paris as he saw it on August 15:[1]

> Reserved seats in the cafés on the Champs Elysées were crammed with Wehrmacht officers drinking beer. At the Cours-la-Reine, a green-clad melancholy soldier, his rifle between his legs, sat between two nursemaids.
>
> On the Place de la Concorde, I saw a white-haired dowager dressed in black and looking very dignified, seated on the luggage rack of a bicycle. The sun-drenched banks of the Seine were black with people. Thousands of Parisians were going for a swim while the battle raged thirty-eight miles away. The famous fisherman of 1814 was still dangling his line at the edge of the bridge.
>
> Along the boulevards Resistance posters were beginning to appear on walls and public urinals; Catholic leaflets denouncing the atrocities of Oradour-sur-Glane were being distributed. Little groups silently gathered on the sidewalk to read the seditious posters.
>
> When I came home I found a notice on the stairway announcing that the gas had been turned off and that all the tenants would therefore have to sign up at a restaurant for the distribution of hot food to carry out.

Electricity was available for an hour and a half only, between 10:30 P.M. and midnight. Economic life gradually ground to a halt. And something unique in Parisian annals occurred— the police went on strike!

---

1. *Mon Journal pendant l'Occupation.*

On August 14 three police organizations belonging to the Resistance met to decide whether to call a strike. Colonel Rol-Tanguy was present. One witness, Lefranc, a member of the Communist-dominated *Front National de la Police,* has recalled the meeting:[2]

> I reminded them that railway and postal workers had already begun their patriotic strike, that in doing likewise the police would be only in third place, and that in any case a patriotic strike by Paris policemen would cleanse them somewhat of the disgrace they had incurred because of the murders committed by the special brigade. Edouard and Durand intervened once again: "Have you considered," they asked me, "the serious consequences of a possible failure?"
>
> . . . Dupuis supported me vigorously. Durand[3] was the first to yield, saying we should all assume full responsibility together. I had the impression that we had won out. This feeling was confirmed when Colonel Rol-Tanguy said: "My military status prohibits me from taking a position on a call for a general strike. However, I must point out that the F.F.I.'s proclamation urging that no more work be done on behalf of the enemy is tantamount to a strike call."
>
> That was it! We had won.

For several days Paris had been the scene of feverish political activity. On August 12 Pierre Laval went to Nancy to see Edouard Herriot, who, under police guard, was being treated at the Malzéville sanatorium. At this moment, however, Herriot was the guest of Bouffet, prefect of the department of the Seine. The last president of the Chamber of Deputies in 1940, Herriot did not reject Laval's idea of convoking the Chamber, but insisted he would do nothing without the concurrence of Jeanneney, President of the Senate. And he was especially leery of Marshal

---

2. *Les Policiers Français dan la Résistance.*
3. *Police et Patrie.*

Pétain. "Bring him back as late as possible, at the very last moment," he told Laval, adding: "I will not shake hands with him."

The Resistance took a dim view of Herriot's presence in the home of a Vichy prefect. Moreover, it was hostile to the 1940 parliamentarians and felt that a return to the old constitutional forms would be an act of treachery.

On this subject, General de Gaulle has observed:

> In spite of the apparent support given to Pierre Laval, his desperate plot seemed to me to lead nowhere. Its success, in the last resort, required my adherence and nothing, not even the pressure of the Allies, could have brought me to admit that the 1940 Assembly was qualified to speak in the name of France.

So concerned were the resisters that they even considered the idea of kidnapping Herriot. As it turned out, when Herriot received more complete information, he rejected any plan that included Pierre Laval.

Pétain, for his part, dispatched Admiral Auphan to Paris with this mandate:

> I hereby empower Admiral Auphan to represent me at the Anglo-Saxon High Command in France and to make eventual contact with General de Gaulle and his qualified representatives on my behalf, in order to find, with regard to French political problems at the moment of the liberation of French territory, a solution of a kind to prevent civil war and to reconcile all Frenchmen of good will.
>
> If circumstances permit, Admiral Auphan will defer to no one before a decision at the governmental level is reached.
>
> Should this prove impossible, I count on him to act in the best interests of our country, provided that the principle of legitimacy which I embody is preserved . . .

Upon learning of Herriot's presence in Paris, Pétain began to fear a parliamentary conspiracy of which he would be the vic-

tim. He was willing to come to Paris, but only if certain conditions were met. De Gaulle paid no attention to his stipulations,
and the Germans removed Pétain from Vichy on August 20.

One after the other, Laval's carefully elaborated plans failed
in the face of widespread hostility. During the night of August
16–17, in response to German demands, members of the Vichy
government who happened to be in Paris at the time left the
capital for Belfort, closely followed by members of the P.P.F.
(*Parti Populaire Français*). On August 17 other notorious collaborationists, with Jean Herold-Paquis in the lead, likewise
hastened to leave.

On the morning of the 18th, Paris no longer had a government. The only ones who remained were prefects, secretaries-
general, and presidents of local assemblies, minus their
assemblies.

Colonel Lizé noted:

> The colonel who headed the F.F.I. of Paris and the Seine
> [Lizé himself] spent the afternoon of August 17 with his chief of
> staff on the Rue Montalivet. . . . Formerly, you could see the red
> flag with the swastika and the black flag of the S.S. from the Rue
> des Saussaies. Now both flags were gone.

The colonel dictated his orders, specifying that all the public buildings in Paris and the environs—ministries, factories,
public service and administrative offices, electrical plants, telephone exchanges, banks, the Métro stations, and water reser-
voirs—were to be occupied on August 18.

That same day, with Raoul Nordling, the Swedish consul
general in Paris, acting as intermediary, an agreement was
reached with the Germans in regard to the liberation of political
prisoners. As a result, 6,000 people were immediately released
in Fresnes, Saint-Denis, la Santé, le Cherche-Midi, Drancy, la
Pitié, and the Val-de-Grâce, yielding places still warm from
their occupancy to the collaborationists. The latter were already
the objects of a purge that was often far from equitable.

On August 18 General Chaban-Delmas, who was serving as the national military delegate in Paris, spoke at length before the COMAC (*Comité Militaire d'Action*). Bringing a message from London, he informed his listeners that General Koenig was opposed to premature intervention by the F.F.I. Operations in Paris must not be allowed to culminate in disaster. Chaban had gone to see the American general Gaffy near Mans on August 13. Gaffy had warned him that the Allies were not planning to occupy the capital for at least another fortnight. He also learned that three or more German divisions, retreating toward the north, would soon traverse the Paris region.

What Chaban-Delmas had to say was not at all to the liking of the extreme leftists who dominated the COMAC. Shortly afterwards, the question was discussed by the Paris Committee of Liberation. Tollett, its president, was a Communist.

Carrel, speaking for the *Front National,* declared, "The time has come to start an insurrection. If you don't want to join us, we'll go ahead without you."

"What will you use for weapons?" Léo Hamon asked.

"We have 600 guns," Rol-Tanguy replied.

"You don't start an insurrection in Paris with 600 guns," Hamon retorted.

But that is exactly what happened. The order to mobilize was issued during the night of August 18–19. Before daybreak, signs were removed from intersections and street corners. Calls for a general mobilization were placarded everywhere. Colonel Lizé noted:

> For the first time, the existence of the Provisional Government of the Republic, the National Council of the Resistance, the Paris Committee of Liberation, and the names of the military leaders were brought to the city's attention.

At an early hour, the Paris police occupied the prefecture. The news of this reverberated like a call to arms. Germans were attacked here and there in the streets. Cars filled with armed youths wearing tricolor armbands roamed about. Public buildings flew the French flag. And "horizontal collaborationists," or, at any rate, women who were suspected of having played that unsavory role, began to have their heads shaved.

Before noon, Charles Luizet, appointed prefect of police by General de Gaulle, took his place in a chair that was still warm from his predecessor, Bussière, who had just been placed under arrest.

Rol-Tanguy wrote:[4]

> I was just getting ready to go to the command post in Denfert-Rochereau, or rather on the Rue Schloelcher—they were connected by an underground passage—when Luizet asked me to join him and Cérat (Alexandre Parodi), the general delegate of the G.P.R.F. [the Provisional Government] in France.
>
> We left immediately for the Avenue de Lowendal to meet Cérat and fill him in on the situation. This done, I obtained his assent to a general mobilization. Cérat placed all Resistance and governmental forces (police, *gendarmerie, garde républicaine*) under my command.
>
> That was a capital decision!
>
> Von Choltitz will feel the effect of this powerful blow. He will realize that a central authority is now in control and that it will be hard to establish liaison between his various bases.
>
> From now on the Germans will be harassed without letup. To be sure, their tanks will attack savagely; but their vacillations, their lack of infantry protection owing to the accuracy of the F.F.I.'s gunfire, have already begun to reveal their deep fear and anxiety. From every porch, from every window, an anti-tank team may emerge, hurling Molotov cocktails that bring death to their targets.
>
> In addition to harassment by mobile patrols, sniping by the *corps franc,* continuous pressure exerted by the entire population, there was the positioning of barricades, those legendary barricades, erected for the purpose of preventing the Boches from getting away.

---

4. *La Libération de Paris.*

Roger Stéphane[5] was on his way to Roger Cocteau's place for lunch that day to celebrate his twenty-fifth birthday. Seeing a big crowd gathered in the Rue de Rivoli, he decided to skip the lunch. After spending some time at the Hôtel de Ville, he went to the prefecture of police, where he was assigned the task of guarding one side of the building. During a skirmish on the Rue Saint-André des Arts, he suffered an arm wound. After getting his arm bandaged at the Hôtel-Dieu hospital, he returned to the prefecture.

The historian Robert Aron has referred to the episode:[6]

> This first hero was asked: "Are you wounded?"
> "Yes, but it's nothing."
> "Would you mind seizing the Hôtel de Ville?"
> "Of course not."
> "Then go ahead."
> The next morning, accompanied by twenty-five men, Lieutenant Roger Stéphane (perhaps he was already a captain) entered the Hôtel de Ville and held it until the arrival of General de Gaulle. According to some, he played a decisive role; according to others, he was merely the fly on the wheel. But, as the good poet Edmond Rostand has written, who knows whether the wheel would ever have climbed the hill had it not been for the fly?

At the radio station, the resisters evicted the general director even though he offered to broadcast messages from the prefecture of police. Parodi ordered all broadcasting shut down in order to prevent the discovery of sending sets. Even appeals to the Allies for help were not sent out over the air. Not until August 22 did the broadcasts resume.

On Sunday morning, operating from the French Office of Information, Claude Bourgeon led the seizure of several build-

---

5. Stéphane, a member of the M.L.N., was arrested and deported in May 1942 but escaped in November. He set up the first service in Paris for the fabrication of false papers. Arrested again in March 1943, he escaped in June.

6. *Historie de la Libération de la France.*

ings on the Place de la Bourse. Printing presses and newspaper offices were now in the hands of the resisters. A batch of new journals, some of them ephemeral, made their appearance: *Ce Soir, Front National, Libération, Combat, Franc-Tireur, Défense de Paris, Libération Soir,* and so on.

The affair of the police prefecture disconcerted the Germans. Von Choltitz told Nordling, "The people of Paris had been described to me as a mob of terrorists, but finding them quite peaceful, I freed a large number of prisoners. Thereupon the terrorists seized the prefecture of police, and now they're firing off their guns all the way to my windows. The French are impossible!"

He weighed the possibility of destroying the prefecture. Above all, he wanted to maintain order. To whom could he appeal? "I won't deal with hooligans and terrorists," he said.

But things were not going so well at the prefecture. Of the 2,000 who had seized the buildings that morning, only about 500 were left by the evening of August 19. And all they had to defend themselves with were thirty-two automatic pistols and rifles.

Over at the headquarters of the general delegation, Chaban-Delmas said he regretted the premature start of the insurrection. Colonel Ely believed that the badly outnumbered F.F.I. could not win. General Bloch-Dassault, the F.T.P.'s military adviser, saw but one way out: to evacuate the prefecture. He said he would try to persuade Rol-Tanguy. To enhance Bloch-Dassault's chances, Parodi appointed him military governor of Paris, a post Chaban-Delmas was happy to relinquish.

To the secretaries-general who had taken over the various ministries, Parodi sent the following urgent message: "The information I am receiving indicates that you have acted too quickly, thus leaving yourselves dangerously unprotected. If you have already proceeded to occupy your ministry, install only a minimal staff and take cover immediately."

The order to evacuate the prefecture of police was transmitted by telephone. But Edgar Pisani and members of the Police Liberation Committee refused to leave the occupied buildings. They decided to take advantage of a temporary respite to get rid of their unarmed comrades. They themselves, bolstered by the possession of at least some weapons, stayed on. Then, at 10:00 P.M., a cease-fire was announced.

With Nordling as a go-between again, contact was maintained with the German staff. The idea of a longer truce gained ground. It was considered on August 20 during a C.N.R. meeting which Parodi, Roland Pré, Generals Bloch-Dassault and Chaban-Delmas, Tollet, and Léo Hamon attended. After a lengthy discussion, the National Council of the Resistance voted in favor of it by a large majority.

Accordingly, during the afternoon, the prefecture's loudspeakers blared the following message: "In view of the German command's promise to spare public buildings occupied by French troops and to treat all Frenchmen in accordance with the rules of war, the Provisional Government of the French Republic and the National Council of the Resistance ask you to hold your fire against the occupying forces until Paris has been completely evacuated. We urge the people to remain calm and to refrain from parking in the streets."

The COMAC, controlled by the Communists, refused to ratify the decision. Rol-Tanguy and Colonel Lizé both reacted in the same way, as it happened. At 2:45 P.M. Lizé even signed a declaration stating that no truce had been concluded and that it was up to him alone to decide about a cease-fire and to so inform his subordinates.

He went on to say that any negotiation with the enemy would be considered an act of high treason, in accordance with existing military regulations, and that as such it would be punishable by death. If necessary, he warned, such punishment would be meted out mercilessly.

At that very moment, Alexandre Parodi, Roland Pré, and Laffon were arrested while driving down the Boulevard Saint-

Germain. Alerted, Nordling intervened to secure their release. That evening, they all met in von Choltitz's office. Parodi announced, "I'm the only Algiers minister on duty here."

Only one thing mattered to the German general. "Are you capable of controlling your men if you make a promise?"

"You are the head of an army. You issue orders. As for me," Parodi said, "I am in charge of a number of different groups. I do not control all of them. The Resistance is spontaneous." And he asked for guarantees.

Von Choltitz replied, "You are in charge of ministries. That's politics. And newspapers are politics, too. Maintenance of the cease-fire is the issue before us. I will order my men not to fire at public buildings. But your men must not fire at my soldiers. And I don't want any barricades."

Von Choltitz noted later: "The interview brought little in the way of results. It seemed clear that the government negotiated by Nordling was no longer respected by the enemy."

But was it respected by the Germans? Von Choltitz's orders, like those of Parodi, were apparently not obeyed.

Colonel Lizé recorded:

> Finally, on the morning of August 21, a meeting was held in the office of the prefect of police. The general delegate of the G.P.R.F. [Parodi] presided. Those present included two members of the COMAC, the commander of the Ile-de-France region, the commander of Paris, and the prefect of police.
>
> After a lively dicussion, the general delegate, speaking as a representative of the G.P.R.F., stated that he would order an immediate truce in Paris and the surrounding suburbs.
>
> Very unhappily, both the commander of the Ile-de-France region and the commander of Paris studied the two itineraries that would be accorded to German troops moving through Paris.
>
> But in many areas the Wehrmacht simply refused to respect the truce. And the S.S. from the very outset rejected it altogether, even launching surprise attacks and torturing or shooting F.F.I. prisoners.

By late afternoon, the commander of the Paris region decided to resume the struggle and to shoot all S.S. prisoners.

At the very moment when the situation was beginning to take a dangerous turn, it became apparent that German directives had toughened. On August 22 von Choltitz received a long letter signed by Hitler. It contained the following order: "Paris is to be turned into a heap of rubble. The commanding general is to defend the city to the last man and to perish if need be beneath the ruins."

Von Choltitz telephoned General Speidel, chief of staff of the army corps stationed near Cambrai, and said, "Thank you for that very fine order."

"What order, my general?"

"Why, the demolition order. Here is what I have decided: I shall call for three tons of explosives for Notre-Dame, two tons for the Invalides, and one ton for the Chamber of Deputies. I am about to blow up the Arc de Triomphe in order to have a clear line of fire. Are you in agreement, my dear Speidel?"

On the other end of the wire, Speidel hesitated, then said, "Yes, my general."

"But you issued the order, didn't you?" von Choltitz asked.

Speidel was indignant. "No! It was the Führer who gave the command!"

Von Choltitz shouted, "Listen, you transmitted that order and you will answer to posterity for it." Then he added: "I'll tell you what I've decided to do: we'll demolish the Madeleine and the Opéra. As for the Eiffel Tower, I'll blow it up in such a way as to block anti-tank guns placed in front of the demolished bridges."

Speidel now realized that von Choltitz was not speaking seriously. With a sigh of relief, he replied, "Ah, my general, how lucky we are to have you in Paris!"

Later, Speidel notified von Choltitz that reinforcements would soon arrive—an infantry division hitherto stationed in

Artois. But this division never reached Paris. Instead, it arrived at Montmorency and Le Bourget very late—on August 26.

It was then that the Führer addressed to German headquarters the famous question: "Is Paris burning?" The query was signed: Adolf Hitler. And we have every reason to believe that he was in dead earnest.

Within the Resistance, meanwhile, advocates and opponents of a truce criticized each other with unprecedented violence and in an atmosphere fraught with drama. Fortunately, in the nick of time, units of General Leclerc's Second Armored Division came to the rescue.

The decision to send them had been reached with some difficulty. Shortly after midnight on August 21, Commander Gallois (Roger Cocteau), F.F.I. chief of staff for the Ile-de-France region, managed to see General Patton at his command post in Courville (Eure et Loir). He filled Patton in on the situation and asked him to send a rescue force to Paris without delay.[7]

Patton replied: "That's impossible. I'm going to talk to you in military terms. It's impossible, and here's why. First, the kind of large-scale military operations we're now undertaking were planned months ago. You know that once plans have been prepared, you've got to carry them out. They can't be changed, even for weighty reasons. Besides, our objective is not to occupy cities, no matter how large they may be. Our aim is to destroy the German army and to be in Berlin as soon as possible."

He continued: "Paris is a very large and heavily populated city. At the rate things are going, to seize a city of that size means that you must accept full responsibility for it. Now, we know that the food supply in Paris is disastrously low. All this would saddle us with a whole series of material and moral responsibilities that had not been anticipated for the current stage of the campaign. We cannot accept such a burden without having taken certain preliminary measures. Finally, it was you, not

---

7. *La Libération de Paris.*

us, who unleashed the Paris insurrection. You thought the right time had come. You alone sized up the situation. If you absolutely needed our help you should have waited for specific instructions from us."

Patton concluded: "All I can say is that the plans I am carrying out do not call for my going to Paris."

Gallois was crushed. The next day, August 22, he went to the town of Laval, where General Omar Bradley had his headquarters. General Sibert, Bradley's chief of staff, received him. Gallois explained the situation.

In a desperate attempt to win him over, I stressed the activities of the Paris Resistance, the importance of the places it had seized, the demoralization of the Germans, who were reduced to asking for a truce, and the absence of organized forces between Paris and the advance lines of the Americans.

A sudden intuition inspired me to end my request with a decisive argument. "The people of Paris now realize what the Resistance has accomplished. They know that there are no Germans in the area around Paris. If an American detachment should fail to occupy Paris at once, Parisians will never forgive the United States for having refused to lend a hand to save their city, which has made such a tremendous effort to assist the Americans."

Colonel Lebel, the French liaison officer who attended the interview, told Gallois afterward, "Your arrival was extremely well timed. For the past two days, two conflicting views have been discussed by our staff officers and by Eisenhower's: Should we continue to carry out without change the plans that had been worked out long ago? Or should we take advantage of this unexpected opportunity and seize Paris virtually without firing a shot—an action that would have not only propaganda value but also worldwide repercussions? Until now the first view has tended to prevail. But your arrival reopened the entire question thanks to the information you supplied. What is so miraculous is that you arrived at precisely the right moment. An hour from now, Bradley will be leaving to confer with Eisenhower. And a definite decision will be reached when they meet. In any event, Leclerc has been summoned here by telephone. We're expecting him at any minute."

Gallois saw Leclerc and recapitulated the information he had brought from Paris. He told Leclerc: "My general, you will have to be in Paris by tomorrow morning."

Leclerc shrugged and said, "An armored division can't be moved just like that. I've cleaned out the Argentan pocket but am still very far from Paris. It would take me three days. I couldn't be there before Saturday."

The French took it for granted that this mission would devolve upon the Second Armored Division. But did the Americans agree?

At 6:30 P.M. Bradley's plane landed at the Laval airfield. A few moments later the general told Gallois, "An important decision has just been reached, and three of us will bear full responsibility for it. First, myself, for I am the one who arrived at this decision. Secondly, General Leclerc, because he will be commissioned to implement it; and third, yourself, because I reached this decision on the basis of your information."

The decision had been made just in time. Already, General Gerow, commander of the Fifth U.S. Corps, to which the Second Armored Division was attached, reacted strongly when Leclerc sent out a detachment on reconnaissance toward Paris. Gerow wrote Leclerc: "This has been done without authorization from the Fifth Corps headquarters and in violation of the orders I issued to your unit.

"I order you to recall this unit to the area near Fleuré where your division is billeted. You will notify headquarters as soon as the detachment has returned to the Fleuré sector. Please acknowledge receipt of this order."

But the rush of events was soon to outdate all this. At his headquarters, Colonel Lizé issued the following directive on

August 21: "The colonel commanding the department notifies all sectors that the truce has been broken and that a fight to the finish must be resumed, this time on an unprecedented scale. Erect barricades all over Paris."

The next day, Colonel Rol-Tanguy posted a fiery proclamation:

> Form groups in every house and neighborhood and combine them into a militia that will be animated by your determination to fight and by your own individual initiatives. Beat up the Boches and seize their weapons. Your actions will hasten the end of the war. Your slogan should be: to everyone his own Boche. No quarter given to the murderers!

The number of bloody encounters increased around the Hôtel de Ville and the Panthéon, in the Cité and the suburbs. On August 22 the German garrisons in the fort at Charenton and in the barracks at Clignancourt ran up the white flag.

On the morning of August 23 everything seemed calmer. But in fact, a telephone message from the Luftwaffe's chief of staff in France informed von Choltitz that preparations were being made to bomb Paris. The attack was to take place that very night, even though plans for the operation were still very vague. General von Choltitz, in an attempt to dissuade the German air force, used a rather curious argument:

> When I asked whether it would be possible at night to hit targets that I myself would select,[8] I was told that the targets would have to be entire neighborhoods. Upon learning this, I threatened to withdraw with my troops because no one could expect me to allow my soldiers to be bombed. I said I would make the Luftwaffe assume that responsibility. I reminded them that my orders specified that I was on no account to abandon Paris. We then agreed that the air attack which had been ordered was not feasible.

---

8. The pilots had asked him to designate the targets.

The afternoon of the 23rd was rather agitated. Colonel Lizé wrote:

> The enemy launched armored attacks, but these were obstructed by hastily erected barricades.
>
> The Germans attacked the police commissioner's office in the Grand Palais and set fire to part of it. Flames and clouds of smoke rose above the central cupola. The enemy shot at the firemen when they appeared. Both sides took prisoners.
>
> An enemy maneuver against the Cité was underway. The Place du Châtelet was attacked. At the Quai du Louvre one of three German tanks moving toward the Cité was destroyed by a Molotov cocktail. Two tanks broke through the barricades on the Pont-Neuf, but a few Molotov cocktails prevented them from going any farther.

Colonel Rol-Tanguy's command post at the Place Denfert-Rochereau was assaulted. The attackers were repulsed, leaving about twenty prisoners in the hands of the F.F.I. Violent skirmishes occurred at the Rome-Batignolles and Villiers-Batignolles intersections.

On August 24, under F.F.I. pressure, the Germans evacuated the armored tower above the Luxembourg.

Alcide Morel[9] has given us the following account of the events of these hours:

> Several times motorized units billed in the Fontenoy area tried to force their way toward the southwest. On the afternoon of the 24th, protected by automatic weapons, a few German units managed to ride the overhead Métro. From time to time they raked the side streets with gunfire. Bullets whistled by.
>
> Breaking through a barricade in the Place Cambronne, one unit got as far as the Rue de la Sablonnière, where it ran into the fire of a SOMUA lorry that had been converted into an armored car.
>
> Armed with pistols, a very few Lebel rifles, and some light

---

9. Co-founder of the "Valmy" Resistance movement.

grenades, our reserves on the Boulevard Pasteur and the Place Garibaldi immediately counterattacked while the four or five submachine guns of the emergency police force and the central commissariat raked the streets. The entire neighborhood became a veritable battlefield.

Defeated, demoralized, the enemy column turned away and returned for the time being to the École Militaire, leaving behind a few prisoners and twenty dead.

As night fell, a German attack, as fierce as it was unexpected, got under way at the Vaugirard slaughterhouse, where the mobile units of the Vaugirard squadron were stationed. The garrison, which had just fought feverishly on the Place Cambronne and in the 14th *arrondissement,* nonetheless held firm.

During the night a German convoy made up of twenty-six vehicles transported munitions and fuel oil down the Rue Croix-Nivert. As it neared the Porte de Versailles, it was intercepted and harassed. After a few detours, it ran into a barricade erected below the railway bridge (397 bis Rue de Vaugirard), which militiamen of the M.L.N. firmly defended, together with members of the "Valmy" and "Convention" groups.

After a brief clash (which cost the life of Georges Walker, a member of the F.F.I.), the Germans branched off into a labyrinth of streets—Cadix, Hameau, Auguste-Chabrière—where barricades and ambushes awaited them. A confused scrap ensued. The firing increased around the obstructed convoy. Georges Dupont and Marcel Guillaumin were felled on the Rue Auguste-Chabrières.

The enemy tried to break away. A Molotov cocktail tossed from a window blew up one of the trucks. The flames spread to the other vehicles as well as to four adjacent shops, causing widespread panic.

The Germans fled. Fifty of them, hidden in cellars, surrendered at dawn.

Night had fallen. The sinister flames from the fire rose like a joyous light. Above us, tracer projectiles fired by German antiaircraft batteries striped the sky and exploded over the southern outskirts of Paris, which Leclerc's advance units had just traversed.

It is now August 24. Ten-thirty at night. Suddenly, the lights have gone on everywhere, and the strains of the *Marseillaise,* of the victorious insurrection, echo endlessly. The distant chimes of Notre-Dame lend a note of gravity to our delight!

An armored division is a large unit. At full strength it comprises 16,000 men, 4,200 vehicles, 200 tanks, 650 cannon, and so on. If formed into a single file the column would be 312 miles long, and it would take twenty-four hours to pass by. Leclerc divided his column into two virtually parallel files until he reached the suburbs of Paris.

On August 23, at about 1:00 P.M., Leclerc was in Rambouillet. He established his command post in the heavy foliage of the park. Lieutenant Bergamain, an officer of the Guillebon detachment, was waiting for him, his uniform stained with blood. He reported that his reconnaissance unit had run into some German tanks on the Trappes road. At this point Guillebon had arrived. Luckier than Bergamain, he had been able to advance as far as Arpajon. Concluding that he would encounter less resistance in the east, Leclerc changed his orders to the fifth corps. His main thrust would be directed against Arpajon rather than Versailles. After conferring with the heads of his tactical units, he made his instructions final at 6:00 P.M.

General de Gaulle had just arrived at the Château de Rambouillet. He summoned Leclerc, who explained the details of his projected attack. The leader of the Free French noted:[10]

> I approved these arrangements and ordered Leclerc to establish his command post at the Gare Montparnasse when he got to Paris. I would join him there in order to decide what to do next. Seeing this young leader already at grips with the battle, and whose courage was complemented by an extraordinary series of well-prepared circumstances, I murmured, "How lucky you are!" I also thought, in war, the luck of the generals is the honor of governments.

10. *War Memoirs,* p. 303.

The mission assigned to Leclerc's men on August 23 was stated quite simply in the operational order: "Seize Paris."

On August 24, Colonel de Langlade's group traversed the Chevreuse and climbed to the plateau of Tousus-le-Noble between the German bases at Trappes-Saint-Cyr and Saclay. Here it ran into a barrage from 88-millimeter anti-aircraft cannon. Commander Massu lost three Sherman tanks but still managed to get through. By then it was 11:00 A.M. The advance continued. The barricades erected by the F.F.I. were quickly dismantled as the group advanced. At 9:35 P.M. Langlade and his men reached the Sèvres bridge. Was it intact? Had it been mined? A tank, preceded by four members of the F.F.I., tried to cross it. Nothing happened. The troops took possession of the opposite bank of the Seine.

Colonel Billotte's unit traversed Arpajon. In Longjumeau it encountered strong resistance but reached Antony around 4:00 P.M. Every intersection was the scene of a skirmish. Colonel Putz's armored cars were blocked at the Croix-de-Berny. Colonel Warabiot's were stopped in front of the Fresnes prison, which had been transformed into a fortress. Two light French tanks were destroyed at the outer edge of the neighborhood. Captain Dupont, leading his men in an attack on the prison, was killed. A tank christened "Notre-Dame de Lorette" dashed down the street a few yards from an 88-millimeter cannon. Struck by a shell, it nonetheless continued on its way, seizing and destroying the German cannon from the opposite side of the street. Another tank entered the prison courtyard, setting on fire the trucks and buses commandeered by the Wehrmacht.

But less glorious episodes also occurred. One such has been described by Lieutenant Bertrand de Chezal:[11]

A teen-age member of the F.F.I., his face covered with pimples, looking like a blackguard, but a very young one, passed by close to us, accompanying a Fritz, his hands on the German's

---

11. *A Travers les Batailles pour Paris.*

neck. For some reason, I happened to glance at the German. He looked furious; there was a nasty sneer on his face. Suddenly, without any provocation—or had the Boche given vent to a muffled bit of arrogance?—the youth pointed his gun at the man. I thought it was all in jest, but he fired! The Fritz flopped down like a limp rag. Without blinking an eye, the pimple-faced adolescent left him and walked off, singing, "She is d-e-a-d!"

I flew into a terrible rage. "It's impossible to tolerate such behavior! We must do something, we must. . . . The Boches will do the same thing to us."

Jean looked at me. "My brother, who was a prisoner, lost his best friend, who was killed in the very same way."

That night, one of Chaban-Delmas's liaison agents, Lieutenant Petit-Leroy, succeeded in finding General Leclerc, who was in Croix-de-Berny. He told the general that von Choltitz would not surrender to the F.F.I., but suggested that he undoubtedly would do so to a high-ranking army officer. The Hôtel Meurice, where the Germans had their headquarters, was the key to the whole affair. On his way back, Petit-Leroy was killed.

Leclerc went up to Captain Dronne. He pointed in the direction of Paris: "Go that way. We've got to enter."

"If I understand you, my general, I'm to avoid any resistance and not bother about what I leave behind me?"

"That's right. Straight to Paris."

The small column left immediately. It comprised three average-sized tanks ("Montmirail," "Romilly," "Champeaubert") and eleven halftracks. From intersection to intersection it drove eastward, entered the capital through the Porte d'Italie, moved down the Boulevard de l'Hôpital, crossed the Austerlitz bridge, and headed for the Hôtel de Ville, which it reached a 10:00 P.M. Dronne spread his tanks and halftracks fanwise around the square.

Inside the hall, Dronne was welcomed by Georges Bidault who embraced him. As the president of the C.N.R. began to speak, there was a burst of gunfire. Everyone flung himself on the floor, then someone looked for the switches to turn off the lights of the chandelier. A little later, Dronne went to the prefecture of police. There he met Chaban-Delmas and Parodi. The latter shouted over the microphone:

"Right before me is a French captain who has just entered Paris, the first to come. His face is red, he's dirty, he hasn't shaved, but I feel like embracing him anyway."

The most exciting night in Paris now commenced. All the church bells were ringing.

From the Hôtel Meurice, von Choltitz phoned his units for the last time. Speidel was on the other end of the line. Standing close to the window, von Choltitz asked, "Do you hear?"

"Yes, I can hear bells ringing," Speidel answered.

"You heard right. The Franco-American army is entering Paris."

"Oh!"

A long silence. Then: "Speidel, what are the army corps' orders for a commanding general who has no troops?"

"You know very well, my general, that we have no orders to issue."

"Let me talk to the field marshal, please."

"The field marshal is standing right next to me at the phone."

"Let me speak to him, please."

"The field marshal is nodding his head. He has no orders to issue."

"In that case, my dear Speidel, there's nothing left to say except good-bye. Take care of my wife and protect her, as well as my children."

"We'll do that, general, we promise you."

The next day, August 25, the bulk of the Second Armored Division entered Paris. One after the other, all the German strongpoints were taken. The "Majestic" command post surrendered to Massu. The toughest fights took place within the block of buildings that included the Ministry of Foreign Affairs, the Presidency of the Chamber of Deputies, and the Palais Bourbon.

The Rouvillois unit lost one tank. The French set fire to one of the ministries where the Germans had dug in. It took five hours to obtain the surrender of the Ecole Militaire garrison—250 men, 50 of whom were killed during the fighting. The tricolor once again flew over the Eiffel Tower and the Arc de Triomphe.

The F.F.I. were also waging heavy battles. Commander Darcourt has described the fighting near the Place de la République:

Group p. 11.35, advancing together with the Léon Piot group, entered the Rue du Faubourg du Temple and the Boulevard Voltaire, bagged a tank and machine gun, and set them on fire. The armored cars would not attempt any more sorties.

Little by little our units drew closer to the square. They got there by going through buildings and over roofs, or crawling alongside of walls. The Germans, trapped by this converging fire while loading their cannon, were killed one by one, or else gave up the fight. Chief adjutant Kamfes killed two cannoneers with two rifle shots.

11:30. Our men have occupied the Métro entrances and are attacking from there. An F.T.P. lieutenant with three comrades, having shot one man firing a 75-millimeter cannon, rushed to the middle of the square, took shelter behind the cannon, and shot down the remaining cannoneer.

Our comrade Barbier [Tergine]—a student promoted to lieutenant—fell, hit in the head by an exploding bullet.

4:30 P.M. Enemy resistance is slackening. All the cannon are silent. Only machine guns in the armored tower of the "Prince Eugène" barracks are still firing. We have occupied all the floors of the Moderne hotel as well as the kiosk. White flags are appearing in the windows of the barracks. At the very same instant, a tank belonging to the Second Armored Division has emerged from the Rue Turbigo and is advancing toward the square in order to parley.

The people of Paris, assuming that the Germans have surrendered, are flooding the square. But the Nazis have opened fire once again.

Our men are returning the fire, and with irresistible dash are overcoming the last German battalion in Paris.

At the Hôtel Meurice the game was up. Von Choltitz has recounted this last episode:

Around two in the afternoon the fighting around us resumed. Tanks opened fire on the hotel, and vehicles parked under the arcades were burned. Resisters, wearing infantry uniforms, followed in the wake of the tanks. The hotel was filled with smoke. Enemy forces entered, tossing smoke bombs into the hall.

After discussing the matter with his officers, von Choltitz agreed to put an end to the fighting. He asked his ordnance officer to go and find a French officer.

Suddenly the door of the adjacent room opened and a haggard, wild-looking civilian rushed in, his finger on the trigger of this pistol. Pointing his gun at me, the man kept asking: "*Sprechen deutsch?*" I calmly answered, "Probably better than you." Whereupon the French officer I had sent my man for, the head of a battalion, entered the room and, sizing up the situation, seized the civilian by the collar and put him out. Then he touched his hand to his cap and asked me in French: "Are you ready to stop the fighting, my general?"

I answered, "Yes, I'm ready." He asked me to follow him, and we left the hotel via a concealed stairway. We walked to my car, which was parked not far away, but the ignition key had disappeared, so we went on foot the rest of the way.

The head of the battalion mentioned by von Choltitz was Commander de la Horie, Billotte's chief of staff. He was accompanied by Lieutenant Karcher. A little later Colonel Billotte himself arrived to take charge of the prisoner and escort him to the prefecture of police.

Once there, von Choltitz was received by Leclerc and Chaban-Delmas. The terms of the surrender were drafted. Then the German general was placed in an armored car and driven to the Gare Montparnasse, where the formal surrender was to be signed.

The text of the capitulation became an object of contention among the French. Kriegel-Valrimont thought the draft unacceptable. Leclerc commanded the Second Armored Division; Colonel Rol-Tanguy commanded the insurgents. Since both forces had contributed to the victory, both leaders were entitled to sign the document. But Leclerc felt that he alone represented all the French forces in Paris. At first taken aback by the dissension, Leclerc nonetheless proved quite conciliatory. The political implications of all this seemed of little matter to him. As a result, the actual text contained a startling anomaly: Colonel Rol-Tanguy's name appeared before that of the man who outranked him, General Leclerc. From a juridical point of view, the entire transaction was flawed by the fact that von Choltitz had not been consulted. For Rol-Tanguy, the right to sign the document represented a purely moral victory.

Around 4:15 P.M. von Choltitz initialed numerous typewritten copies of the following statement: "Resistance within and around Paris must cease immediately."

The German commander of greater Paris noted:

My officers, accompanied by those of the 1st French army [he was obviously alluding to the Second Armored Division], were dispatched to every part of the city with this order. Unfortunately, in the process of carrying out their mission, they became the object of so many personal attacks and insults that it proved difficult to find officers willing to go out on such an errand a second time. Some copies of the text were taken to sectors well outside of Paris, where the troops were not subject to my orders. They promptly arrested my officers as well as the French soldiers who accompanied them.

While all this was taking place, the American 4th infantry division, in turn, entered Paris and took over the attack on the Gare de Lyon and Vincennes.

Both generosity and gratuitous cruelty highlighted this day. Some devoted themselves to caring for the wounded, others howled for revenge. There were a few dramatic scenes. At the Place de l'Etoile a woman rushed up to one of the prisoners and put out his eye with a pin. At the Place des Pyramides a volley of machine-gun fire from a tank decimated a column of prisoners. But hatred focused mainly on female "collaborationists" or on women merely suspected of having collaborated—for many mistakes were made.

The historian Adrien Dansette has noted:[12]

The most spectacular victims are women, most of them accused of a too intimate collaboration. Shoved about by shrieking hordes, there they are, many of them wearing simple blouses, a few entirely undressed, their faces convulsed, their heads shaved except for a ridiculous tuft in the shape of a swastika. Some have swastikas painted on their foreheads or backs. Occasionally the droll is combined with the tragic in such a way as to overshadow it. A case in point is the adventure of a young woman from Boulogne-Billancourt whose charms carried a tariff. Beaten by the virtuous citizens, she kept whimpering her personal but imperfectly understood credo: "My ----- is international, but my heart is French."

At 4:30 P.M. General de Gaulle arrived at the Gare Montparnasse. By five he was at the Ministry of War, where he installed himself and his staff. At 7:15 he went to the Hôtel de Ville, where he delivered a speech calling for national unity.

"The nation will never allow this unit to be broken," he said. "The nation knows that to conquer and rebuild, to become great, it must have all its children with it."

---

12. *Histoire de la Libération de Paris.*

The C.N.R. met that night. Many of its members expressed surprise that the Republic had not yet been proclaimed. Political differences began to surface even before the country was completely liberated.

On August 27 Leclerc, in a letter addressed to de Gaulle, detailed his impressions without mincing words:

> An enormous majority of the population, especially in Paris, magnificently French and national, wants only one thing: to be commanded in order to rebuild France (there is everywhere a yearning for authority).
>
> F.F.I.—A general assessment. Like the Partisans at the time of the war in Morocco, ten out of every one hundred are very good, very brave, true fighters; twenty-five to thirty out of one hundred follow the example of these men. The rest are useless or worse.
>
> Heads of the F.F.I. Today I had some interesting talks with F.F.I. officers who fought effectively. They told me that the *Front National* had tried in every way to exploit French enthusiasm for the benefit of the "Party." They did not succeed.
>
> The leaders, even though appointed by our government, are very timid. This, I believe, is the crux of the problem. The matter is of no concern to me personally. I am a soldier and nothing else. But, having witnessed a few scenes, I feel I must report them to you. Your task will not be made easy, my general.

The liberation of Paris and its suburbs was not entirely completed until August 28. Figures for the period since August 18 showed 1,062 dead (532 members of the F.F.I., 130 of the Second Armored Division, 400 civilians); 7,024 wounded (1,005 members of the F.F.I., 319 soldiers of the Second Armored Division, 5,700 civilians).

On September 2 members of the Provisional Government, who had landed at Cherbourg after a rough crossing from Algiers aboard the cruiser *Jeanne d'Arc,* arrived in Paris. The city was once again the capital of France. Here the Fourth Republic would be established.

CHAPTER FOURTEEN

IN CONCLUSION:
A NEW ROLE

I N Brittany as in Normandy, in Provence and in southwestern France, on all the roads leading to Paris as well as in the capital itself, the forces of the Resistance were on the attack in the summer of 1944. Whether carrying out individual acts of sabotage, skirmishing in small numbers, or throwing their weight by the thousands into the great battles that were gradually driving the enemy from their country, the Resistance fighters proved even to the skeptical Americans the imposing and vital nature of their role.

But that role had obviously changed. From its fragmentary, isolated beginnings, at a time when secrecy was of the essence, the Resistance had emerged as a full-scale, nationwide military movement. The maquisards traversing all of France with such ardor were no longer guerrillas. Their groups had gradually become regular, solidly organized units, with their own services and even their own field hospitals. Now the problem was how to integrate them into the new French Army.

The day after Lyon was liberated, General de Lattre de Tassigny stated in an interview published in the newspaper *Le Patriote:*[1]

> Never will we totally absorb the F.F.I. It is indispensable to preserve their name, their mystique, the pride of their units. In view of the present condition of our wartime army, it would be most unadvisable to alter the structure of the F.F.I. Either individually or in organized groups that preserve their individuality, members of the F.F.I. are voluntarily joining our army. As soon as circumstances allow, some sort of synthesis must be effected between what they represent and what we represent, and this must be done with maximum reciprocal understanding. To all the values and qualities they have acquired as fighters, we will ask them to contribute an effort directed toward order and discipline, so that the country may recognize them as a reconstituted part of the army of tomorrow.

A decree of September 23 stipulated that all men who were still under arms would have to sign up in appropriate fashion for the duration of the war. General de Gaulle remarked in his *War Memoirs:*

> Thus the situation of the maquisards would be legally settled. Forty thousand were transferred into the Navy and the Air Force. To assist the Minister of the Interior to maintain public order, those *gendarmes* and *gardes mobiles* who had joined the maquis would return to their original groups; besides, sixty *"Compagnies Républicaines de Sécurité"* were formed, an innovation universally criticized at the time but still in existence today. Finally, certain specialists of whom the nation's economy stood in the greatest need—miners, railway men, etc.—were requested to return to

1. Issue of September 9, 1944.

their professions. Ultimately, the land army alone retained more than 30,000 soldiers who had spontaneously transferred to it from the Forces of the Interior.

According to de Gaulle, General de Lattre took about one hundred thousand members of the F.F.I. The rest were organized into seven new divisions: the 27th in the Alps, under Valette d'Osia; the 10th in Paris (Billotte); the 19th in Brittany (Borgnis-Desbordes); the 25th, comprising the maquisards in contact with the German pockets, in Saint-Nazaire, La Rochelle, Royan, Pointe-de-Grave (Chomel); the 23rd (Anselme); the 1st in the Berri (Callies); the 14th in Alsace (Salan). The last two were formed in the spring of 1945.

Recalling the integration of the F.F.I. into the army, de Lattre wrote in his *Histoire de la Première Armée française:*

I know that I have sometimes been reproached for my "weakness" for the F.F.I., for the time I devoted to them, including nights spent receiving visits from twenty-eight-year-old colonels. . . . It is true that at the time I sometimes kept men waiting who outranked them. But these men were privileged beings who waged war—magnificently—with everything that was needed to do so. The others were "unfortunates" who had to be convinced or comforted, often distrustful, sometimes incompetent, almost always generous, behind whom a heroic and unsullied youth had gathered, the very elite of our adolescence who willingly fought without shoes, almost with their bare hands. They have proved by their attitude that my confidence in them was justified.

INDEX